Samuel Manning, Richard Lovett

The Land of the Pharaohs

including a sketch of Sinai, drawn with pen and pencil

Samuel Manning, Richard Lovett

The Land of the Pharaohs
including a sketch of Sinai, drawn with pen and pencil

ISBN/EAN: 9783337096496

Printed in Europe, USA, Canada, Australia, Japan

Cover: Foto ©Andreas Hilbeck / pixelio.de

More available books at **www.hansebooks.com**

THE

LAND OF THE PHARAOHS

INCLUDING A

SKETCH OF SINAI

𝔇rawn with 𝔓en and 𝔓encil

BY THE

REV. SAMUEL MANNING, LL.D.

AUTHOR OF 'THOSE HOLY FIELDS,' 'SWISS PICTURES,' ETC.

NEW EDITION REVISED AND PARTLY RE-WRITTEN

BY

RICHARD LOVETT, M.A.

AUTHOR OF 'NORWEGIAN PICTURES,' 'PICTURES FROM HOLLAND,' ETC.

THE RELIGIOUS TRACT SOCIETY

56 PATERNOSTER ROW AND 164 PICCADILLY

1887

'No two countries in the world offer so many claims on the attention of the Christian inquirer as *Palestine* and *Egypt*; the promised land and the house of bondage, the holy and the unclean, the type and gate of heaven, and the image of a world that lieth in wickedness. In the Old Testament they are at once connected and opposed, like the Church and the world under the Gospel. The allegory is continued into the New Testament, which opens with the announcement, "Out of Egypt have I called My Son." If the student of Holy Scripture gives the first place in his inquiries to the land of the Law and the Prophets, the mountains and valleys which echoed the daily psalmody of the temple, the scenes of the Saviour's life and miracles and passion,—the second place is as naturally claimed by the nation from the midst of whom the chosen people were brought out " by a mighty hand and by a stretched out arm ; " a land that sheltered Israel from the famine, and Jesus from the sword.'

Canon Trevor.

TOMBS OF THE CALIFHS, CAIRO.

PREFACE TO THE NEW EDITION.

THE first edition of this book has been before the public for some years. Written with all the original author's brightness and skill, and dealing with one of the most fascinating countries on the globe, it deserved, as it has attained, a high place in the popular regard. The lamented death of Dr. Manning, in 1881, prevented him from undertaking the work of revision that had become necessary in the course of years. Increased facilities for travel, many new discoveries illustrative of the ancient Egyptian life, the recent development of Egyptian scholarship, and the growth in number and greater excellence in quality of engravings, depicting Egyptian people and places, have all combined to render a new edition of the book desirable.

The public events of recent years have also tended to deepen the general interest in Egyptian matters. In fact, Egypt has a curious power of keeping herself well to the front in the international relations of the various European nations. In 1878, the obelisk, which now adorns the Thames

Embankment, and upon which the eye of Moses probably rested once and again during his Egyptian life, was brought to England. In the following year Ismail Pasha abdicated, and the state of affairs reached a position which soon led to active interposition on the part of England. The crisis came in 1882. In June riots broke out in Alexandria, and large numbers of Europeans left the city. On July 11th, Alexandria was bombarded, and the forts silenced. War followed, and on September 12th Arabi Pasha was defeated at Tel-el-Kebir, and banished. In the same year Professor Palmer was murdered by Bedouins in the Sinai region.

In 1883 the troubles connected with the Mahdi began, and in 1884 the total rout of Hicks Pasha's army led to General Gordon's mission to Khartoum. This was followed by the British Expedition up the Nile for his rescue. In 1885 the battle of Abu-Klea was fought, the expedition failed to reach Khartoum in time, and that city was taken by the Mahdi, Gordon losing his life. Soon after this the Mahdi also died, and the English troops retired to Assouan.

Very naturally, this series of events did not pass without wide differences of opinion as to the policy and the justice of the part played by England. The extremes are represented, on the one hand by those who hold that we had no right to go near Egypt at all; and on the other by those who think that we ought to take Egypt and govern it 'in the interest of the natives,' as we have done in India. But with all such divergencies of view we have nothing to do here. We allude to the series of events only because it is impossible in any work on Egypt to ignore them. The blood and treasure we have spent during the last ten years in that ancient land have necessarily deepened the interest felt in it by all thoughtful readers. Deeds of bravery and heroism have not been lacking, whether we deem them to have been done in a righteous cause or not. And this volume, in its new and improved form, will help to make clear to those at home the land and the people on whose behalf they were done.

The two chief events throwing light upon ancient Egypt have been carefully noted in this new edition. The first is that marvellous discovery at Deir-el-Bahari in 1881, by which we are enabled to look upon the mummied faces of mighty Egyptian Kings and Queens who flourished at the period of, and even long before the Exodus. The other is the establishment of the Egypt Exploration Fund, which bids fair to do useful work in the way of exploring ancient sites.

The editor's object has been to alter the original work as little as possible. Lapse of time had rendered some statements obsolete, and had compelled the modification of others. The only entirely new portion is Section IV., which deals with events that have happened since the last edition was printed. A considerable number of the old illustrations have been omitted, and their space has been occupied by fifty-four of the best recent engravings illustrative of Egyptian natives, scenery, architecture and antiquities.

The editor has also to express his grateful acknowledgments to Mr. E. A. Wallis Budge, M.A., of the department of Oriental Antiquities in the British Museum, not only for many valuable hints, but also for reading the proof sheets of a large part of the work.

In this new and revised form, the 'Land of the Pharaohs' is sent forth with the hope that it may tend to satisfy that desire for knowledge about the oldest kingdom in the world, which every intelligent general reader feels, and which is especially needful and interesting to the devout Biblical student.

R. LOVETT.

VIEW ON THE NILE NEAR PHILÆ.

IN THE STREET OF CAIRO

· LIST · OF · ILLUSTRATIONS

SECTION I.

ALEXANDRIA TO CAIRO.

SECTION II.

CAIRO TO ASSOUAN.

SECTION III.

ASSOUAN TO ABU-SIMBEL.

SECTION III. (*continued*).

SECTION IV.

RECENT DISCOVERIES IN EGYPT.

SECTION V.

THE SUEZ CANAL.

SECTION VI.

EGYPT TO SINAI.

THE STEPPED PYRAMID AT SAKKARA.

ALEXANDRIA TO CAIRO.

GENERAL VIEW OF CAIRO, WITH THE PYRAMIDS IN THE DISTANCE.

A Street in Cairo.

SECTION I.

Alexandria to Cairo.

IN the dim grey dawn of a February morning, I was on the deck of the Austrian steamer *Urano*, peering eagerly through the mist to the southward. The clear crystalline blue of the Mediterranean had changed to a greenish grey, showing that we were in shallow water. As the sun rose, the haze vanished, and we could make out the coast line, a long stretch of sand, here and there broken by a hillock, a clump of palm-trees, an Arab village, or the white walls and dome of a *santon's* tomb. Then a forest of masts came into view, and, rising above them, a venerable column and a lighthouse. The column we recognise as Pompey's Pillar; the lighthouse is the modern representative of the famous Pharos of Alexandria, one of the wonders of the ancient world. We were approaching that mysterious land which had attained a high civilisation, and a settled monarchy, when Abram 'went forth from Ur of the Chaldees, to go into the land of Canaan.'[1] It was in its glory when the Hebrews were there held in bondage. It had passed its prime when David and Solomon sat upon the throne of Israel. It had sunk into decay when Rome rose to power, and at the dawn of modern history it had ceased to exist as a nation. Hebrew patriarchs, Greek philosophers, Persian, Macedonian, and Roman conquerors, have all been drawn hither, and its annals are inextricably interwoven with theirs. It played an important part in the greatest event in our world's history, when Joseph 'arose and took the young Child and His mother by night, and departed into Egypt: and was there until the death of Herod: that it might be fulfilled which was spoken of the Lord by the prophet, saying, Out of Egypt have I called My Son.'[2] In later ages the land of the Pharaohs is ever coming into prominence. Amongst the early Christians, Cyril, and Athanasius, and Origen; amongst the early Mohammedans, Amrou and Omar; amongst the Crusaders, St. Louis of France, and Saladin, the chivalrous enemy of Richard Cœur de Lion, all lead our thoughts to Egypt. What wonder, then, that it was with a feeling of almost reverential awe, that I first gazed upon the soil which, for four thousand years, had been the scene of so many memorable deeds?

POMPEY'S PILLAR.

The gravity of those of our party who were for the first time visiting Mohammedan countries, was somewhat disturbed by the appearance of the pilot who now came alongside. His dress was a curious combination of eastern and western attire, very characteristic of the mongrel population of Alexandria. It consisted of a Turkish fez, an Arab *abba*, baggy linen knickerbockers, and a pair of

[1] Genesis xi. 31.   [2] Matthew ii. 14. 15. Hosea xi. .

AN EGYPTIAN DONKEY-BOY.

unmistakable English boots with elastic sides. legged on the gangway of the steamer, pipes and coffee were served, and he steered us through the intricate channel into the harbour of Alexandria. The usual scene of confusion now ensued. Scores of boats came round us, manned, as at Jaffa, by half-naked negroes and Arabs. I was seized by half-a-dozen fellows at once, each endeavouring to appropriate me. A similar conflict was going on over every article of my baggage, and it was only by a vigorous application of the dragoman's whip that I and my belongings were rescued from them and stowed away in one of the boats.

We only escaped from the hands of the boatmen to fall into those of the donkey-boys, who effectually dissipated whatever feelings of reverence yet remained. These Arab lads are surely the cleverest and most impudent little urchins on earth. Our city-Arabs cannot compare with them. In broken English they vaunt the praises of their animals : 'Take my donkey ; him berry good donkey ; him name Billy Barlow.' If the traveller be

Having seated himself cross-

AN EGYPTIAN DRAGOMAN.

presumably an American, the sobriquet is changed to 'Yankee Doodle.' One ingenious youth, whose only garment was a ragged cotton shirt, through which his tawny skin showed conspicuously, having tried 'Billy Barlow,' 'Champagne Charley,' and half-a-dozen names besides, made a final appeal, by exclaiming, 'Him name Rosher Tishburne ; him speak English ; him say, "How you do, sar?"' It was impossible either to lose one's temper or retain one's gravity amid this merry, clamorous crowd. At length we extricated ourselves from them and made our way to the hotel.

DONKEY-BOYS AT ALEXANDRIA.

Anywhere, except in Egypt, Alexandria would be regarded as a very ancient city. Its history goes back more than two thousand years, to the time of its founder, Alexander the Great, B.C. 333. But here, this venerable antiquity seems quite modern. It is a mere *parvenue*, which sprang up when the kingdom of the Pharaohs had run its course and reached its close. It is now a busy thriving port in which the east and west meet in strange confusion. Nubians, Arabs, Berbers, Greeks, Italians, French, English, Circassian pilgrims, Lascar sailors, Chinese coolies, jostle one another in the crowded streets. A string of camels pass with their burdens into the railway station. A Bedouin sheikh takes a ticket for Cairo, or wrangles over the price of a piece of Manchester goods. Hadjis from Mecca are waiting to go on board the steamer bound for Constantinople or Beirout. Sailors from the harbour, or soldiers *en route* for India, shoulder their way through the bazaars. Go into a bank or counting-house, and you might fancy yourself to be in the heart of London. Step out into the street, and you see a devout Mussulman spreading his prayer-carpet in the roadway, and performing his devotions, as little disturbed by the bustle around him as though he were alone in the desert.

The northern coast-line of Egypt is a sterile waste, consisting of little else than salt swamps, lakes of brackish water, and barren sand. The importance and prosperity of Alexandria are therefore due, not to the surrounding district, but to the fact that it is the port for the only African river which flows into the Mediterranean. Regions of boundless fertility stretch southward to the equator, through which the Nile flows and forms their sole means of communication with the sea. To the ancient world, Alexandria, which lay near the mouths of this mighty river, formed the meeting-place of eastern and western civilisation—the emporium of European, Asiatic, and African commerce. With the downfall of the Byzantine Empire, its glory departed. The Mohammedan conquest fell like a blight upon its prosperity, and the discovery of the route by the Cape of Good Hope gave the death-blow to its commerce. For many generations

CLEOPATRA'S NEEDLES AS THEY WERE PRIOR TO 1880.

it was little more than an obscure village of the Turkish Empire. During the present century it has again been rising into importance. Its present population is estimated at a quarter of a million. In the year 1883, its exports reached upwards of twelve millions sterling, its imports seven and a half millions. The opening of the Suez Canal diverted the through traffic to India into the new channel. But other causes have since been at work, which have more than made up for the loss thus sustained, and the population and commercial prosperity of the city are rapidly increasing.

There are few remains of the ancient splendour of the city of Alexander the Great and the Ptolemies. Pompey's Pillar and Cleopatra's Needles have no right to the names they bear. The former was erected by Pompeius, prefect of Egypt, in honour of the Emperor Diocletian (A.D. 302). The monoliths of red syenite granite, covered with hieroglyphics, known as Cleopatra's Needles, formerly stood at Heliopolis, where they were raised by Thothmes III., a Pharaoh of the eighteenth dynasty.[1] They were removed to Alexandria by one of the Cæsars, and are doubtless the same which Pliny described as standing in front of the Cæsarium. One of them has been removed to New York; the other, presented to the British nation by Mohammed Ali, was brought to this country and placed upon the Thames Embankment at the cost of Dr. Erasmus Wilson in 1877.

THOTHMES III.

From the Bust in the British Museum.

On the downfall of the Hebrew monarchy, Alexandria became a new home to the exiled Jews. They so greatly increased in wealth and numbers, that at one period they formed a third of the whole population of the city. Numerous synagogues were built in the cities of Lower Egypt, and a temple upon the plan of that at Jerusalem was erected in the nome of Heliopolis. It was for the use of these Hellenistic Jews that the Septuagint translation was made, which had so important an influence in preparing the way for the introduction of the Gospel, by making the Old Testament Scriptures known to the Gentile world. The history of this version is obscured by myth and legend. All that is known, with certainty, is that the translators were Alexandrian Jews, and that it was completed under the patronage of Ptolemy Philadelphus.

[1] The mummy of this great monarch was discovered at Deir-el-Bahari in 1881. See Section IV. of this volume, also *Cleopatra's Needle*. *By-paths of Bible Knowledge*, No. 1, pp. 119-121.

A remarkable case of deliverance from persecution, and of punishment coming upon the persecutors, is recorded of the Jewish colony at Alexandria. Ptolemy Philopator (B.C. 217), being incensed at the refusal of the high-priest to admit him into the temple at Jerusalem, returned to Egypt and cast into prison all the Jews upon whom he could lay his hands. Those of Alexandria were confined in the Hippodrome, a vast amphitheatre used for gladiatorial shows and public games. The king ordered that they should be trampled to death by elephants, made furious by wine and stimulating drugs. For two days the execution was delayed by the drunken carousals of the king. This interval was spent by the prisoners in ceaseless prayer to God for deliverance. On the third day the savage beasts were driven into the arena and urged upon the prisoners. But, instead of attacking them, they turned upon the guards and spectators, many of whom were killed, the rest fleeing in terror. Ptolemy was so impressed by this manifestation of the Divine power that he ordered the prisoners to be released, restored their privileges, and, as in the days of Esther and Ahasuerus, gave them permission to kill their enemies.

The journey from Alexandria to Cairo is now almost always made by railway, a distance of one hundred and twenty-eight miles. The road first skirts the shores of Lake Mareotis, with myriads of pelicans, wild ducks, and other water-fowl swimming or wading in its brackish waters, or soaring in dense clouds overhead. The narrow strip of desert which forms the northern coast-line of Egypt is soon crossed, and we enter the Delta of the Nile, which continues almost as far as Cairo. The soil, a deposit of Nile mud, is of extraordinary fertility. The Delta used to be regarded as the granary of Rome. Innumerable vessels were employed in conveying the wheat grown in this district to the imperial city. In one of these the Apostle Paul was wrecked, and in another he completed his voyage to Italy as a prisoner.[1] The river formerly ran through it in seven channels. Five of these are now dried up, and two only remain, known as the Rosetta and the Damietta branches. The change was foretold by the prophet Isaiah: 'The Lord shall utterly destroy the tongue of the Egyptian sea, and with His mighty wind shall He shake His hand over the river, and shall smite it in the seven streams, and make men go over dryshod.'[2]

It seems certain that the eastern portion of the Delta was the land of Goshen, in which the patriarchs were settled on their coming down into Egypt. It lay between Canaan and the residence of Joseph at On, or Heliopolis, for, on receiving tidings of the arrival of his father, 'Joseph made ready his chariot, and went up to meet Israel his father, to Goshen, and presented himself unto him.' From the marvellous fertility of the soil it was well suited for a pastoral people, it was 'the best of the land.' Though belonging

---

[1] Acts xxvii. 6-38 : xxviii. 11.

[2] Isaiah xi. 15 ; xix. 5. The literal fulfilment of this prophecy becomes still more apparent when it is remembered that the two mouths still remaining are artificial, not natural channels.

THE RUINS OF TAVIS.

to the Egyptian monarchy, and used as a pasture-ground for Pharaoh's cattle, it did not form part of Egypt Proper. Hence, it was allotted to a shepherd race, where they lived without coming into offensive contact with the native population, 'for every shepherd is an abomination to the Egyptians." It is probable that yet another reason for the settlement of his brethren in this frontier province suggested itself to the sagacious mind of Joseph. The nomad races of Palestine were, about this period, a serious peril to the Egyptian monarchy. The mysterious Hyksos, or shepherd kings, were a Canaanitish horde, who poured across the Isthmus, and, for a time, established themselves as conquerors in the Nile Valley. Whether this invasion had already taken place, or whether it was now an object of alarm, may be doubted. But, in either case, the location of a band of hardy and warlike herdsmen on the frontier, to bear the brunt of the first assault, was a piece of policy worthy of the wisdom of the illustrious Grand Vizier, who had already saved his adopted country from the horrors of famine.

The most interesting city of this district was T'săn, which in Hebrew becomes Zoan, in Greek Tanis, and in Arabic Săn. Tanis in all probability is referred to in Numbers xiii. 22, where we read, 'Now Hebron was built seven years before Zoan in Egypt,' and in Psalm lxxviii. 12, 'Marvellous things did He in the sight of their fathers, in the land of Egypt, in the field of Zoan.' For ages it was a great and powerful city, and at one period was the chief centre of the Hyksos power. A king named Apepi III. was ruling there when Ra-Sekenen of Thebes (the recent discovery and unwrapping of whose mummy is referred to in Section IV.) led the national movement which resulted in the expulsion, eighty years afterwards, of the shepherd kings. Tanis was captured finally by Aahmes I., and the hatred felt by the Egyptians towards the foreign dynasty which had so long ruled them led them to mutilate or destroy all existing monuments of the Hyksos rule, which had extended over a period of 511 years.

Until 1798 the site of Tanis was unexplored, and in that year it was only surveyed by the French engineers ; but between 1815 and 1836 many of its antiquities were carried off and sold to wealthy collectors. In 1860, Mariette uncovered the temple ruins, and in so doing revealed an enormous number of most valuable remains. The engraving depicts the site of Tanis at the time of his excavation. In 1884, Mr. Flinders Petrie explored the site anew under the direction of the Egypt Exploration Fund. Although productive of no exceptional discoveries, many most valuable antiquities were thus brought to light.[2]

In 1883, the same society sent out M. Naville to explore what was then known as Tel-el-Maskhutah, and was supposed to be the site of the ancient Raamses. M. Naville claims to have proved by his excavations

---

[1] Genesis xlvi. 28-34 ; xlvii. 1-6.
[2] See an interesting paper by Miss Edwards, in *Harper's Magazine* for October, 1886.

that the site is Pithom, the ancient store city built by the Israelites, and
that it is identical with Succoth, Pithom and Succoth being only different
names for the same place. These results have not been accepted as final
by all Egyptologists, but they all tend to increase our knowledge of what
was anciently the Land of Goshen.[1]

GIRLS COMING TO THE NILE FOR WATER.

As the train bears us slowly, and
with frequent stoppages, over the
district where the sons of Jacob
pastured their flocks and herds, we have abundant opportunities for observing
the habits of the people. A wide expanse of verdure stretches to the very
verge of the horizon. Groups of fellaheen, or peasantry, are seen sitting
under the shadow of a palm grove, or lounging by the wayside, utterly
indifferent to the intense heat, which makes the atmosphere quiver like the

[1] See *The Store City of Pithom, and the Route of the Exodus.* By E. Naville.

mouth of a furnace. Veiled women, clad only in a blue cotton skirt, come down to the river to fill their water-jars, and then, poising them on their heads, walk away with a firm, graceful step. A family pass along the road; the husband, a big, stalwart fellow, rides a donkey; the wife, bearing a load which would be heavy for an English porter, walks by his side; a group of brown naked children run alongside the train holding out their hands and crying for backsheesh, and in this cry their elders join them whenever they have an opportunity. Notwithstanding this universal begging, I saw little or no actual destitution in Egypt. The wants of the peasant are so few, and the soil is so productive, and so easily cultivated, that everybody, even the very poorest, seems to be well fed. Fuel costs nothing; and drink, the curse of European countries, is unknown. A draught of Nile water, a handful of lentils, or a piece of bread, made like a pancake, and tough as wash-leather, are all that his necessities demand. Give him a little oil or vinegar, an onion or two, and a cup of coffee, and he feasts luxuriously. A careful observation of the condition of the fellaheen convinced me of the accuracy of Miss Martineau's remarks: ' I must say that I was agreeably surprised, both this morning and throughout my travels in Egypt, by the appearance of the people. About the dirt there can be no doubt; the dirt of both dwellings and persons, and the diseases which proceed from want of cleanliness; but the people appeared to us, there, and throughout the country, sleek, well-fed and cheerful. I am not sure that I saw an ill-fed person in all Egypt. There is hardship enough of other kinds, abundance of misery to sadden the heart of the traveller; but not that, so far as we saw, of want of food. I am told, and no doubt truly, that this is owing to the law of the Korân, by which every man is bound to share what he has, even to the last mouthful, with his brother in need; but there must be enough, or nearly enough, food for all, whatever be the law of distribution. Of the progressive depopulation of Egypt for many years past, I am fully convinced; but I am confident that a deficiency of food is not the cause, nor, as yet, a consequence. While I believe that Egypt might again, as formerly, support four times its present population, I see no reason to suppose, amidst all the misgovernment and oppression that the people suffer, that they do not raise food enough to support life and health. I have seen more emaciated, and stunted, and depressed men, women and children in a single walk in England, than I observed from end to end of the land of Egypt.'[1]

Though the Delta is not so entirely rainless as many parts of the Nile Valley, yet the productiveness of the soil is mainly dependent on artificial irrigation. The water left by the annual inundation is stored up in canals and reservoirs, and distributed over the soil by various devices. Sometimes a large wheel is run out into the river and turned by the force of the

[1] *Eastern Life, Present and Past.* By Harriet Martineau, vol. i. p. 9.

current. The floats of the wheel are made hollow, so as to take up a quantity of water. As they rotate, and begin to descend, the contents of each are poured out into a trench, or tank, rudely constructed on the bank.

A more common method is the sakich. In every part of Egypt we may see a rude roof of thatch under which a camel or buffalo plods round a worn path, turning a series of wheels cogged and creaky, drawing up an endless and dripping string of earthen vessels, which splash out their crystal gatherings into one leaky and common pool; and thence, along a moss-clad shaft, into a little babbling rill of pure water flowing off on a bounteous errand. The groaning and creaking of these sakiehs is one of the most familiar sounds on the Nile. It becomes associated, in memory, with hot, sultry afternoons, spent in delicious indolence on the deck of a dahabeah, gliding downward with the current; with cool evenings, when the stars come out in the deep blue of an Egyptian sky, to shine with a lustre unknown in our northern latitudes; less pleasantly associated with restless nights, when the boat has been moored near one of these machines, and the incessant noise combines with rats, mosquitoes, fleas, and innumerable other plagues of Egypt to banish sleep.

SAKIEH.

More common than either is the shadoof, a primitive contrivance consisting only of a long pole working on a pivot, a lump of clay, or a stone fixed at one end, a bucket at the other. For hundreds of miles up the Nile the river is lined with these shadoofs; men, women, and children, either absolutely naked, or with only a strip of cloth round their loins, spending their whole lives in lifting water out of the bountiful river to irrigate their fields. No wonder that the ancient Egyptians worshipped the Nile, and that it needs all the force of Mohammedan iconoclasm to prevent the fellaheen of to-day from worshipping it too. The very existence of Egypt, as we shall see hereafter, is absolutely due to the river. Were its beneficent current to fail, or its mysterious inundation to cease, Egypt would again

FELLAHEEN AT WORK IN EGYPT.

become a part of the desert from which it has been reclaimed, and which hems it in on either hand.

The distribution of water over the soil is effected by means of trenches leading into small channels, these again into yet smaller gutters. Each plot of land is divided into squares by ridges of earth a few inches in height. The cultivator uses his feet to regulate the flow of water to each part. By a dexterous movement of his toes, he forms a tiny embankment in one of the trenches, or removes the obstruction, or makes an aperture in one of the ridges, or closes it up again, as the condition of the crop requires. He is thus able to irrigate each square yard of his land with the utmost nicety, giving to it just as much or as little water as he thinks fit. This mode of cultivation is very ancient, and was probably referred to by Moses, when, contrasting the copious rainfall and numerous fountains of Palestine with the laborious irrigation of Egypt, he said, 'For the land, whither thou goest in to possess it, is not as the land of Egypt, from whence ye came out, where thou sowedst thy seed, and *wateredst it with thy foot*, as a garden of herbs : but the land, whither ye go to possess it, is a land of hills and valleys, and drinketh water of the rain of heaven.' [1]

Though the trains on Egyptian railways are probably the slowest and most irregular in the world, yet some progress is made, and, in the course of a few hours, it becomes evident that our destination cannot be far distant. The broad expanse of verdure narrows as the Delta approaches its southern apex at Cairo. The tawny line of desert which bounds it on either side draws nearer. The Libyan and Mokattam ranges of hills, which inclose the Nile Valley, come into view. Then, those who know where to look for them, may make out, through the quivering haze, at a distance of ten or twelve miles, the most extraordinary group of buildings in the world. In approaching almost any other object of interest for the first time—St. Peter's at Rome, for instance, or Mont Blanc—there is a brief interval of hesitation and doubt before its definite recognition. But at the very first glance, without a moment's pause, we exclaim, *The Pyramids !* They are at once the vastest and the oldest buildings on the earth. They were standing, perhaps were even already ancient, when Abraham came down into Egypt. Their origin was lost in the recesses of a remote and legendary past, when the Father of History conversed with the priests of Saïs and Memphis. It may have been bombast, but it was scarcely exaggeration, when Napoleon, on the eve of the battle of the Pyramids, issued his famous *ordre du jour*, 'Soldiers, forty centuries are looking down on you!' And now, by a strange anachronism, we are gazing quietly out of the window of a railway carriage, at edifices which seem to be nearly coeval with the existence of man upon the earth.

[1] Deuteronomy xi. 10, 11.

But our reveries are broken in upon by our arrival at the railway station, where a struggle like that at Alexandria awaits us with the *hammals* and donkey-boys contending for the possession of our persons and baggage. Having extricated ourselves from their clutches with some difficulty, we make our way to the hotel.

Cairo lies at the entrance of the Nile Valley, near the point at which the river branches out into the channels which form the Delta. Its modern name is a European corruption of that given to it by its Arab conquerors—*El Kaherah*, the victorious. By the natives it is called *Misr* or *Masr*, and the same name is given by them to the whole of Egypt. This is evidently a modern form of the Scriptural Mizraim, and affords another instance of the survival of ancient names through a long course of centuries,

LATTICE WINDOWS IN CAIRO.

and after repeated conquests by foreign nations.[1] It is situated about a mile from the river. A long straggling street leads down to Bûlâk, which is the port; and Fostat, or Old Cairo, runs along the Nile bank. The population of the city was given in the census of 1882 as 368,108, but good authorities reckon it as 400,000 in round numbers. The resident Europeans amount to 21,000.

Those who wish to see the Cairo of romance, and of the *Arabian Nights' Entertainments*, should lose no time in visiting it, for it is being rapidly 'improved off the face of the earth.' The new quarter is but a shabby reproduction of modern Paris, from which all characteristic Oriental features—the graceful lattice-work windows, the overhanging stories, the picturesque colour—have disappeared. The Ezbekeeyah garden has nothing but its semi-tropical vegetation to distinguish it from the public gardens of any European capital. Young Egypt, sallow-faced, and dressed in fez cap, baggy, ill-fitting black clothes, and patent leather boots, unsuccessfully affects the airs, and only too successfully cultivates the vices, of Parisian *flâneurs*. Said Pasha, who died in 1863, greatly benefited Egypt by his administrative skill and enlightened policy; but since his day the old picturesque life of the East has been fast passing away, and a thin veneer of European civilisation has been superimposed upon unalloyed native barbarism. That the sanitary condition of the city was horrible, and that improvement was

---

[1] See for numerous parallel instances *These Holy Fields*, p. 89.

urgently needed, cannot be questioned. If the Khedive had set himself to effect the necessary reforms by developing a system of architecture in harmony with the habits of the people, the requirements of the climate, and the characteristics of Arabian art, he would have done a good work. But the new Boulevards satisfy none of these requirements. They are simply poor imitations of a faulty original. And this applies to the whole system of administration. It is an exotic which has no roots in the soil, and no adaptation to surrounding conditions.

But, as an American gentleman said to me, 'Cairo is a big place, and can stand a great deal of improving.' In a few minutes we may pass from the Frank quarter into the labyrinthine windings of bazaars, which are almost unchanged since the days of Saladin, and in which 'Haroun Alraschid, Giaffar, the Grand Vizier, and Mesrour, the chief of the eunuchs,' might have wandered and found little to surprise them. The Mooskee affords us a good line of transition from the one to the other. We enter the main thoroughfare, broad for an Eastern city, with a Bavarian *bier-halle* at one corner, and at the other a shop for the sale of French books and photographs. The roadway is, of course, unpaved, but it is wide enough to allow a carriage to drive along it, with space for foot-passengers on either side. Each carriage is preceded by its running footmen—lithe, agile fellows, who can keep ahead of the horses, going at full speed, for an incredible distance. They wear a light dress

AN EGYPTIAN FOOTMAN.

of white linen, which leaves the arms and legs bare. Each carries a wand by day, a flambeau by night. Their duty is to warn pedestrians to get out of the way, which they do by incessant cries : 'To the right.' 'To the left.' 'Look out in front,' mingled with good-humoured abuse of those who are slow to take their warnings. Lines of camels [1] with their long swaying necks, soft, silent tread, and peevish groans, stalk solemnly

[1] Barham Zincke's description of the camel, though long, is too good not to be quoted : 'Its long neck is elevated and stretched forward. It is carrying its head horizontally, with its upper lip drawn down. In this drawn down lip, and on its whole demeanour, there is an expression of contempt—contempt for the modern world. You can read its thoughts. "I belong," it is saying to itself, for it cares nothing about you, still you can't help under-

A MINARET IN CAIRO.

along the middle of the roadway. A string of donkeys, surmounted by inflated balloons of black silk or white muslin, from which dainty little slippers of red or yellow morocco leather peep out, are carrying the ladies of a harem to take the air. Here comes a procession of blind men chanting the Korán, followed by a group of women wailing and crying in tones of well-simulated grief; between them is a board carried on men's shoulders and covered by a pall, beneath whose folds it is easy to make out the rigid lines of a corpse on its way to the cemetery. Shrill gurgling cries fall upon the ear, taken up and repeated by the female bystanders, perhaps with the accompaniment of a hautboy and a drum or two. It is a marriage procession. The bride, a mere child ten or twelve years of age, swathed from head to foot in red or yellow shawls, and inclosed in a canopy or tent, is being conducted to the

standing it, " I belong to the old world. There was time and room enough then for everything. What reason can there be for all this crowding and hastening? I move at a pace which used to satisfy kings and patriarchs. My fashion is the old-world fashion. Railways and telegraphs are nothing to me. Before the Pyramids were thought of, it had been settled what my burden was to be, and at what pace it was to be carried. If any of these unresting pale faces (what business have they with me?) wish not to be knocked over, they must get out of the way. I give no notice of my approach; I make way for no man. What has the grand calm old world come to? There is nothing now anywhere but noise and pushing and money-grubbing; " and every camel that you will meet will be going the same measured pace, holding its head in the same position, drawing down its lip with the same contempt, and soliloquising in the same style.'—*Egypt of the Pharaohs and the Khedive.*

bath or to her husband's house.¹ Veiled women, black slaves, Bedouin sheikhs, burly pashas, water-carriers, blind beggars, Greek and Coptic priests, donkeys and their drivers, and street-sellers innumerable, make up the picturesque and bewildering throng.

The street-sellers in their number and variety would demand a chapter to do them justice; and to interpret their cries requires a far greater knowledge of Arabic than I possess. They form, however, so important and characteristic a feature in the aspect of an Eastern city, that they cannot be altogether passed over. I avail myself, therefore, of Mr. Lane's help in the matter. 'The cries of some of the hawkers are curious, and deserve to be mentioned. The seller of "tirmis" or (lupins) often cries, "Aid! O Imbábee! Aid!" This is understood in two senses; as an invocation for aid to the sheikh El-Imbábee, a celebrated Muslim saint, buried at the village of Imbábeh, on the west bank of the Nile, opposite Cairo, in the neighbourhood of which village the best tirmis is grown; and also as implying that it is through the aid of the saint above-mentioned that the tirmis of Imbábeh is so excellent. The seller of this vegetable also cries, "The tirmis of Imbábeh surpasses the almond." Another cry of the seller of tirmis is, "O how sweet the little offspring of the river!" The seller of sour limes cries, "God make them light" (or easy of sale). The toasted pips of a kind of melon called "abdalláwee," and of the watermelon, are often announced by the cry of "O consoler of the embarrassed! O pips!" A curious cry of the seller of a kind of sweetmeat ("haláweh"), composed of treacle fried with some other ingredients, is, "For a nail, O sweetmeat!" He is said to be

A CAIRENE WOMAN AND CHILD.

half a thief; children and servants often steal implements of iron, etc., from the house in which they live, and give them to him in exchange for his sweetmeat. The hawker of oranges cries, "Honey! O oranges! honey!" And similar cries are used by the sellers of other fruit and vegetables, so that it is sometimes impossible to guess what the person announces for sale, as when we hear the cry of 'Sycamore-figs! O grapes!' except by the rule that what is for sale is the least excellent of the fruits, etc., mentioned; as sycamore-figs are not as good as grapes. A very singular cry is used by

¹ I saw a curious illustration in the streets of Cairo of the irresistible innovations of the West, and the unchanging customs of the East. The bride was being taken home in a *cab*, but the canopy was tied over the roof, and fixed to the four corners, to represent the four poles which usually support it.

the sellers of roses : " The rose was a thorn ; from the sweat of the Prophet it blossomed." This alludes to a miracle related of the Prophet. The fragrant flowers of the henna-tree are carried about for sale, and the seller cries. " Odours of Paradise ! O flowers of the henna !" A kind of cotton-cloth, made by machinery which is put in motion by a bull, is announced by the cry of " The work of the bull ! O maidens ! " [1]

A familiar cry in the streets of Cairo is that of the water-carrier. Sometimes he uses almost the very words of the prophet Isaiah : ' O ye thirsty, water ! ' He does not, however, go on to say, ' without money and without price ; [2] but for a small coin, less than an English farthing, he fills one of the brass cups which he chinks incessantly as he walks along. A more ambiguous cry, but one in common use is, 'Oh, may God compensate me ! ' More frequently he exclaims, ' The gift of God ! ' recalling the words of our Lord, speaking to the Samaritan woman of the Holy Spirit :

A STREET IN CAIRO.

' If thou knewest *the gift of God*, and who it is that saith to thee, Give Me to drink ; thou wouldest have asked of Him, and He would have given thee living water.' [3]

[1] *Manners and Customs of the Modern Egyptians.* By E. W. Lane, pp. 318, 319.
[2] Isaiah lv. 1.   [3] John iv. 10.

As we leave the Mooskee behind us, and enter the purely native quarter, the streets become narrower, till at length a laden camel can scarcely pass, its burden touching the wall on either side. The upper stories of the

A WATER-SELLER.

houses, which project as they ascend, almost meet overhead, leaving only a narrow strip of sky visible. But even yet we have not penetrated into the innermost arcana of the bazaars. I was several days searching for the

A STREET IN CAIRO.

goldsmiths' bazaar before I could find it. At length, passing out of a very narrow street, through a dark and filthy archway, I found myself in a gloomy passage, in which it was impossible for two persons to walk abreast. On either side the goldsmiths were busy, each with his charcoal fire, blowpipe and anvil, producing the exquisite jewellery for which Cairo is so justly famous. Filigree work, fine as the finest lace, jewelled necklaces and nose rings, head-dresses inlaid with diamonds and pearls, were offered for sale, in dirty holes and corners, by men black with the smoke of the forge at which they had been working. There was no display of wealth. Every article was brought out separately, and its price fixed by weight. Yet even here the intrusive West had made its way. Each

INTERIOR OF THE MOSQUE OF THE SULTAN HASAN.

jeweller had at the back of his forge an iron safe made in London or Birmingham, in which his treasures were stored.

BAB EZ-ZUWELEH OR BAB EL-MUTAWELLEE, CAIRO.

The mosques in Cairo are very numerous, not fewer, it is said, than four hundred. Many of them are of considerable size and architectural

merit. But, with the single exception of that of Mohammed Ali, recently
erected, they are all falling into dilapidation. Many reasons are assigned for
their ruinous condition. It is said that the Egyptians are deterred from
repairing them by superstitious feelings. Others ascribe the neglect to a
decay of religious faith and zeal. The more probable explanation is, that
the government having confiscated the estates of the mosques, as well as

SANCTUARY OF THE MOSQUE OF IBN-TOOLOON.

those of private individuals, now fail to discharge the duty of keeping the
edifices in repair. The mosque of Sultan Tooloon is interesting to architects
from the fact, that although built a thousand years ago (A.D. 879), it had
pointed arches at least three hundred years before their introduction into
England. That of Sultan Hassan, near the citadel, is a building of great
beauty, constructed out of the casing stones of the Great Pyramid. ' It

VILLA AND GARDEN NEAR CAIRO.

abounds,' says Fairholt, 'with the most enriched details of ornament within
and without; not the least remarkable of its fittings being the rows of
coloured glass lamps hanging from its walls, of Syrian manufacture, bearing
the Sultan's name, amid glowing coloured decorations; they are some of the
finest early glass-work of their kind, but many are broken, and others hanging
unsafely from half-corroded chains.' Though this mosque is the boast and
pride of the Cairenes, yet it is allowed to remain in a condition of filth and

COFFEE-HOUSE IN THE SUBURBS OF CAIRO.

dilapidation which seems to prove that all religious zeal is dying out from
the hearts of the people.

The suburbs of Cairo, and the surrounding district, are very interesting.
Weeks may be spent in visiting and revisiting the many points of attraction.
In the environs are charming villas, each standing in a garden, rich in all
the products of a semi-tropical country, and abundantly supplied with water.
As we ramble in the outskirts of the city, we often come upon an open space
occupied as a fair. How like, and yet how unlike, an English fair! Swings
and round-abouts are here, but dark-skinned, bright-eyed Arab youngsters

have taken the place of our 'young hopefuls.' Yonder is a serpent-charmer with necklace and girdle of snakes; before him are half-a-dozen puff-adders, erect upon their tails, and waving to and fro with a rhythmic motion to the music of a rude guitar. Near him sits a story-teller, reciting in guttural Arabic some interminable tale from the *Thousand and One Nights*, the group seated round him listening with a fixed attention which nothing seems to weary. Jugglers, mountebanks, and acrobats are performing their feats precisely as we see them at home. Booths, constructed with a few poles and rafters, over which a vine has been trained, afford shadow to loungers who sit hour after hour, sipping coffee or sherbet, and listening to the dismal tones of a *tarabookah* or Nubian drum, a reed pipe, and a dulcimer. It is a merry, and yet a sad scene. These men are mere children, with no occupation for the present; no care, or purpose, or hope, for the future.

Continuing our ramble along the banks of the Nile, we cross a branch of the river to visit the Nilometer. It was built in the year 716 A.D. by order of the Caliph Suleiman, and has been restored many times since that date. A pit lined with masonry is sunk to the level of the bed of the river, but the lower part is choked with mud and with the remains of the dome, which has fallen in. A graduated column rises in the centre indicating in cubits the height to which the inundation reaches. The sixteenth cubit is called the Sultan's water, as the land tax is only levied when this height is attained. It is notorious that the official and the true record never agree. 'A good Nile,' as it is called, is from eighteen to twenty-two cubits. Less than this leaves the soil insufficiently irrigated; more than this drowns the country and inflicts immense mischief upon the peasantry. Every morning during the rise of the river criers go throughout Cairo proclaiming the level to which the inundation has reached. The announcement is awaited with intense and eager interest, for upon it depends the question whether the coming year shall be one of famine or of abundance. When the proper height has been attained the dams are cut, allowing the water to flow into the canals, and universal rejoicings prevail throughout the city.

Perhaps there is no place in the immediate vicinity of the city which is visited and revisited with deeper interest than the Citadel. It stands on a rocky eminence which rises to the east of Cairo, and commands a magnificent view extending over the city, the desert, and far down the Nile Valley. In this wonderful view the Pyramids form the most impressive feature. Though clearly visible, and within easy reach, they stand quite apart from the surrounding landscape. The narrow strip of cultivated soil along the banks of the river approaches, but does not touch, them. The solitude and silence of the desert broods over them. The noise from the city at our feet falls upon our ears. Its busy life moves beneath our eyes. But nothing breaks in upon the sense of awful mystery and separation from the existing world which invests these venerable monuments of antiquity.

A tragic interest attaches to one of the courts of the Citadel. In 1811 Mohammed Ali learned that the Mamlukes intended to rebel against him.

THE NILOMETER.

He therefore invited their chiefs to be present in the Citadel on the investiture of his son Toossoom Pasha with the command of the army.

Upwards of 400 came. The ceremony over, on mounting their horses to ride away, they found the gates closed. At the same moment, a fierce fire of musketry was opened upon them from the windows of the surrounding barracks. Resistance and escape were alike impossible. They galloped

THE CITADEL AT CAIRO.

round the narrow inclosure, seeking in vain to find a way of escape or an enemy whom they might attack. Men and horses fell in heaps in the court-yard. Only one of them, Emin Bey, survived. He leaped his horse over the precipice which forms the western front of the Citadel. The animal was killed by the fall, but he escaped as by a miracle, and reached a camp

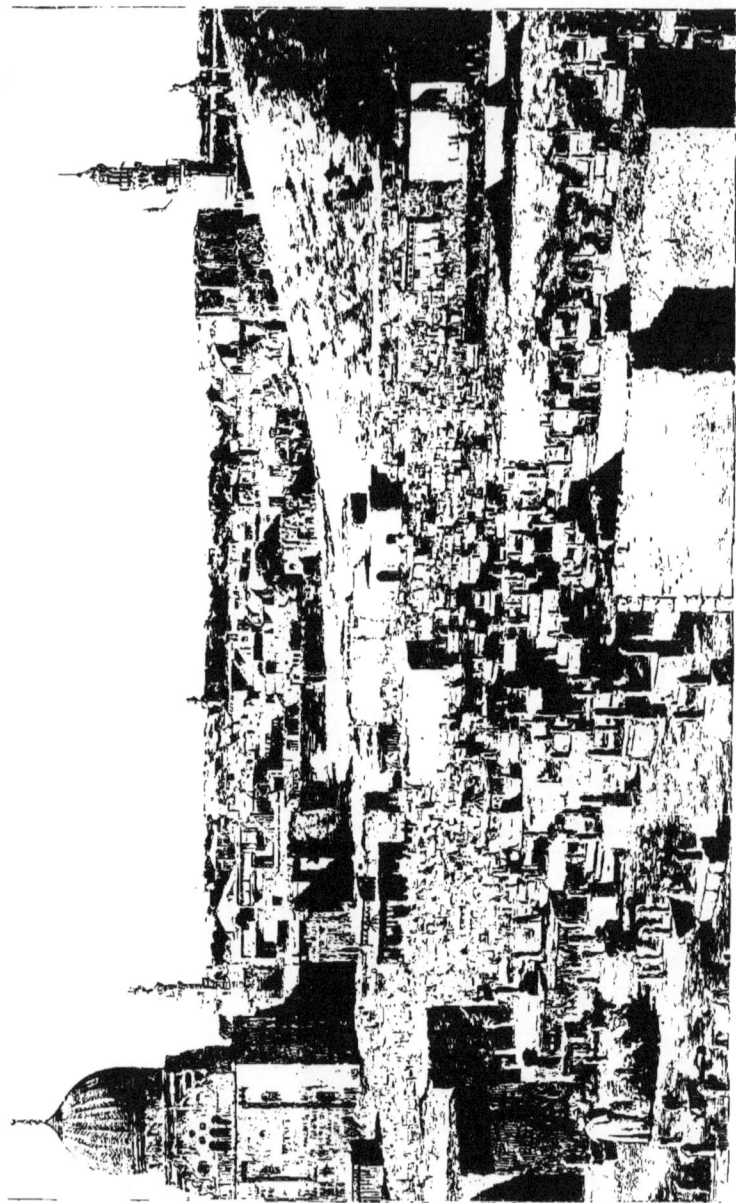

The Cemetery and Tombs of the Caliphs, Cairo.

of Arnauts in the plain below, who refused to surrender him to the Pasha; and he succeeded in making his way from the country in disguise. The soldiers who had taken part in the massacre were rewarded by being permitted to plunder the houses of their victims and to complete the ex-termination of the Mamlukes by slaughtering those who had not been present at the ceremony. Upwards of twelve hundred are said to have perished. As we visit the splendid Mosque of Mohammed Ali, close to the scene of the massacre, it is impossible not to remember with horror this frightful tragedy.

Though few or none of the remains of the Egypt of the Pharaohs are to be found in Cairo, yet it stands in close proximity to some of the most impor-tant cities of the ancient dynasties. The site of Memphis, which we shall visit on our journey up the Nile, is only a few miles to the south. Helio-polis is still nearer. Pass-ing out from the city, and leaving the Citadel and

MOSQUE OF MOHAMMED ALI IN THE CITADEL.

the tombs of the Caliphs on our right, the road leads, under avenues of tamarisk and acacia, through a richly-cultivated district. Soon, however, the limits of vegetation are reached, and we enter upon the vast tract of sand which bounds Egypt on every side. The line of fertility and barrenness is not, however, continuous and unbroken. Wherever a depression in the soil or an extension of irrigation brings the waters of the Nile to a point in advance of the ordinary limit of cultivation, there the desert 'rejoices and blossoms as the rose.' In one of these projecting points of fertile soil, immediately before we reach the site of the ancient city, is a garden, in the midst of which stands a venerable sycamore tree, hollow, gnarled, and almost leafless with extreme age. It is enclosed by palisades, and is regarded with veneration by the Copts as the place where Joseph, Mary, and the infant Saviour rested on their flight into Egypt. The fact that there was a great Jewish settlement in this neighbourhood gives a certain measure of plausibility to the legend. The tree itself, though evidently of great age, cannot be as ancient as the legend affirms.

The road now leads through a wide plain, covered with a luxuriant growth of sugar-cane. From amidst the broad green glossy leaves a single column of red granite rises, covered from summit to base with hieroglyphics. It is the sole relic above the soil of the once famous City of the Sun—the Heliopolis of Herodotus and Strabo, the Bethshemesh of Jeremiah,[1] the On

THE OBELISK OF USERTESEN I. AT HELIOPOLIS.

of Joseph.[2] To this great university city of ancient Egypt, Plato, Eudoxus, and the wisest of the Greeks, came to be initiated into the mystic lore of the priests. Here, as Manetho tells us, Moses was instructed in all 'the learning of the Egyptians.' This solitary column, raised about a century before the time of Joseph, looked down on his marriage with 'Asenath, the daughter of Potipherah.' It has stood in its present position for nearly four thousand years, and is the sole survivor of the avenues of sphinxes, the temples and palaces, and colleges and obelisks, described by Greek historians. Even in Egypt we shall visit few spots invested with a deeper and more various interest than this.

[1] Jeremiah xliii. 13.   [2] Genesis xli. 45.

But the great excursion from Cairo yet awaits us—that to the Pyramids. I had seen them so frequently from a distance, and had been so deeply impressed by their solemn and solitary grandeur, that it was with an apprehension of disappointment that I started in the early morning to spend a long day in examining them more closely. Until recently, the trip was not without some difficulty. The Nile had to be crossed by a ferry; donkeys were the only means of conveyance; and the traveller must often go some miles out of his way to avoid a canal or a tract of land under water, or he

THE PYRAMIDS.

must be carried over it on men's shoulders. Now a noble bridge is thrown across the river, and a broad highway, above the reach of the inundation, leads under an avenue of carob trees, past the Viceroy's palace, to the very foot of the plateau on which the Pyramids stand. Lovers of romance and adventure complain of the change, and they hear with dismay that a branch railway is talked of. It is certainly a very prosaic affair to drive out to Gizeh in a carriage and pair, with as little risk or trouble as is involved in a trip to Richmond. But for those who have only a

E

single day to devote to the excursion, the new road is not without its advantages.

In about an hour after leaving the Ezbekeeyah, we see the Pyramids rising from the sandy plain, evidently close at hand. The first view is certainly disappointing. They are much smaller, and also much nearer, than we had supposed. Two hours was the time allotted for the journey thither, yet our watches show that only one has passed. We soon discover that we are under an optical delusion. The perfect clearness of the air, the want of any intervening objects to break the monotony of the plain, or to mark the distance, and the immense size of the Pyramids themselves, had led us to suppose that we had reached our destination when less than half of the distance had been traversed. As we sped on our way, they loomed larger and larger before us, till at length, when we found ourselves at the foot of the plateau, they fully realised all our expectations. I, at least, felt nothing of the disappointment and disenchantment to which many travellers have given expression.

Vast and imposing as are the Pyramids even at the present day, it is important to remember that we do not see them in their original condition. It has been said that, 'All things dread Time; but Time itself dreads the Pyramids.' The destructive agency of man, however, has effected what mere natural decay was powerless to accomplish. The huge masses of masonry are indeed proof against the assaults alike of man and of time. But as originally constructed, they offered not the rough and broken outline up which we now climb, but a smooth and polished surface, perhaps covered with hieroglyphics. For centuries they furnished quarries out of which modern Egyptians have built their cities. Though their beauty has been thus destroyed, their bulk is not perceptibly diminished. Abd-el-Atif, an Arab physician, writing in the twelfth century, when the casing stones were yet in their places, says : 'The most admirable particular of the whole is the extreme nicety with which these stones have been prepared and adjusted. Their adjustment is so precise that not even a needle or a hair can be inserted between any two of them. They are joined by a cement laid on to the thickness of a sheet of paper. These stones are covered with writing in that secret character whose import is at this day wholly unknown. These inscriptions are so multitudinous, that if only those which are seen on the surface of these two Pyramids were copied upon paper, more than ten thousand books would be filled with them.' One of these inscriptions is said by Herodotus to have recorded that sixteen hundred talents of silver were expended in purchasing radishes, onions, and garlic for the workmen ; reminding us of the complaint of the Israelites : 'We remember the fish, which we did eat in Egypt freely ; the cucumbers, and the melons, and the leeks, and the onions, and the garlic.'[1]

---

[1] Numbers xi. 5. The general opinion of Egyptologists is that the Pyramids were without hieroglyphics. The statements of Abd-el-Atif and Herodotus, however, are so precise, that it seems difficult to doubt them.

DISTANT VIEW OF THE PYRAMIDS.

E 2

If, as we stand upon the plateau of Gizeh, now covered with mounds of ruin and débris, we would picture to ourselves the scene which it presented in the time of the Pharaohs, we must conceive of the three Pyramids as huge masses of highly-polished granite, the area around them covered with pyramids and temples, amongst which the Sphinx rose in solemn, awful grandeur to a height of a hundred feet. What is now a silent waste of desert sand would be thronged with priests, and nobles, and soldiers, in all the pomp and splendour with which the monuments make us familiar, while just below us, stretching along the Nile, the palaces of Memphis glittered in the sun. As we realise to ourselves this magnificent spectacle, we may understand something of the self-denial manifested by Moses when 'he refused to be called the son of Pharaoh's daughter;' and of his dauntless courage when he stood before the king, and demanded that he should 'let the people go.' It was only as 'by faith he endured, as seeing Him who is invisible,' that he was able to rise to this height of heroism; 'choosing rather to suffer affliction with the people of God, than to enjoy the pleasures of sin for a season; esteeming the reproach of Christ greater riches than the treasures in Egypt: for he had respect unto the recompence of the reward.'[1]

The following are the dimensions of these stupendous monuments, as measured by Mr. Perring.[2]

	1st Pyramid.		2nd Pyramid.		3rd Pyramid.	
	Present.	Original.	Present.	Original.	Present.	Original.
	Feet.	Feet.	Feet.	Feet.	Feet.	Feet.
Sides of the base . .	746	767	690	705	352	352
Slant height . . .	568	614	563	577		283
Perpendicular height .	450	479	447	457	203	219
Angle of elevation . .	--	51·20	—	52·21	--	51·10
Area of the base, sq. yards	61.835	65.437	53.015	55.320	13.853	

The Great Pyramid is, therefore, more than half as long again on every side as Westminster Abbey, and, though deprived of more than thirty feet by the removal of its apex, it is still fifty feet higher than the top of St. Paul's, and more than twice as high as the central tower of York Minster. It covers thirteen acres of ground, equal to the area of Lincoln's Inn Fields, and is computed to have contained 6,848,000 tons of solid masonry.

The pyramid itself contains two chambers, which have received the appellation of the *King's* and *Queen's*. The latter is lined with slabs of

---

[1] Heb. xi. 24 27.

[2] Baron Bunsen has justly pointed out that, in their present state of dilapidation, no admeasurements, however carefully taken, are more than an approximation.

polished stone, very carefully finished, and artistically roofed with blocks leaning against each other to resist the pressure of the mass above. This apartment is reached by a sloping passage, which terminates in a gallery or hall twenty-eight feet high. From the entrance to the gallery a horizontal passage, one hundred and nine feet long, leads to the 'queen's chamber,' which measures seventeen feet (north and south) by eighteen wide, and is twenty feet high to the top of the inclined blocks.

SECTION OF THE GREAT PYRAMID FROM NORTH TO SOUTH.
1. SUBTERRANEAN VAULT.   2. QUEEN'S CHAMBER.   3. KING'S CHAMBER.

The gallery continues to ascend till it reaches a sort of vestible, which leads to the 'king's chamber.' This chamber is finished with as much care as the other, and measures thirty-four feet by seventeen, and nineteen in height. The north and south walls are pierced by two shafts or tubes, about eight inches square, slanting up through the entire fabric to the exterior of the pyramid.

The 'king's chamber' contained a red granite sarcophagus without a lid; it was empty, and had neither sculpture nor inscription of any kind. The door was guarded by a succession of four heavy stone portcullises, intended to be let down after the body was deposited, and impenetrably seal up the access. The roof of the chamber is flat; and, in order to take off the weight above, five spaces, or *entresols*, have been left in the structure. On the wall of one of these garrets, never intended to be entered, General Vyse discovered, in 1836, what had been searched for in every other part of the pyramid in vain. Drawn in red ochre, apparently as quarry marks on the stones previously to their insertion, are several hieroglyphic characters, among which is seen the oval ring which encircles the royal titles, and within it a name which had already been noticed on an adjoining tomb. On the latter it was read *Shufu* or *Chufu*, a word sufficiently near, in the Egyptian pronunciation, to *Cheops*, whom Herodotus gives as the founder of the largest pyramid.

Cartouche of Cheops.

One of the most singular features in this pyramid is a perpendicular shaft descending from the gallery in front of the 'queen's chamber' down to the entrance passage underground, a depth of 155 feet. The workmanship shows that this well was sunk through the masonry *after* the completion of the pyramid, in all probability as an outlet for the masons, after barring the sloping ascent with a mass of granite on the inside, which long concealed its existence. The lower opening of the well was closed with a similar stone; the builders then withdrawing by the northern entrance, which was both barricaded and concealed under the casing, left the interior, as they supposed, inaccessible to man.

These extraordinary precautions go to confirm the tradition related by Herodotus, that Cheops was not buried in the vault he had prepared, but secretly in some safer retreat, on account of violence apprehended from the people. As no other pyramid is known to contain an upper room, it seems not improbable that the 'queen's chamber' was the refuge where his mummy lay concealed while the vault was broken open and searched in vain.

Lepsius has shown that the Pyramids were constructed by degrees. The vault was excavated, and a course of masonry laid over it, in the first year of the king's reign. If he died before a second was completed, the corpse was interred, and the pyramid built up solid above. With every year of the king's life an addition was made to the base as well as to the superstructure, so that the

VIEW OF GALLERY IN THE GREAT PYRAMID, FROM THE LOWER AND UPPER LANDING-PLACES.

years of the reign might have been numbered by the accretions, as the age of a tree by its annual rings. When the last year came, the steps were filled out to a plane surface, the casing put on, and the royal corpse conveyed through the slanting passage to its resting-place.

The Second Pyramid stands about 500 feet to the south-west of the First, and is so placed that the diagonals of both are in a right line. It is somewhat smaller, but stands on higher ground. The construction is similar to the other, save that no chamber has been discovered above ground. It was surrounded by a pavement, through which a second entrance, in front of the northern face, descends deep into the rock, and then rises again to meet the usual passage from the regular opening in the face of the pyramid. From the point of junction a horizontal passage leads to a vault, now called by the name of Belzoni; it measures forty-six feet by sixteen, and is twenty-two feet in height. It is entirely hewn in the rock, with the exception of the roof, which is formed of vast limestone blocks, leaning against each other and painted inside. When discovered, this vault contained a plain granite sarcophagus, without inscription, sunk into the floor. The lid was half destroyed, and it was full of rubbish. Some bones found in the interior turned out to be the remains of oxen; but the sarcophagus was not large enough to admit more than a human mummy. Besides the large vault, Belzoni found a smaller one, eleven feet long, and a third, measuring thirty-four feet by ten, and eight feet five in height, but neither contained any sepulchral remains.

BUST OF CHEPHREN IN THE MUSEUM AT BOOLAK.

The general workmanship of this pyramid is inferior to that of the larger one. It retains its outer casing for about 150 feet from the top, and is, consequently, more difficult of ascent. No name has been found on any part of the Second Pyramid, and its erection is not mentioned by Manetho. A tradition preserved by Diodorus assigned it to Amasis; but an adjacent tomb contains an inscription to a royal architect, in which the monarch is called 'Shafra the Great of the Pyramid,' and this has been supposed to be *Chephren*, the brother of Cheops, to whom Herodotus ascribes the Second Pyramid.

Cartouche of Chephren.

The Third or Red Pyramid—so called from the colour of the granite casing which covered the lower half, and has protected its base from diminution—is described by the classical writers as the most sumptuous and magnificent of all. It certainly surpasses the other two in beauty and regularity of construction. It covers a suite of three subterranean chambers, reached as usual by a sloping passage from the northern face. The first is an anteroom twelve feet long, the walls panelled in white stucco. Its door was blocked by huge stones, and when these had been removed, three granite portcullises, in close succession, guarded the vault beyond. In this apartment, which measures forty-six feet by twelve, and is nearly under the apex of the pyramid, a sarcophagus had apparently been sunk, but none remained. The floor was covered with its fragments (as Perring supposed) in red granite;

and Bunsen ascribes the fracture to Egyptian violence. Others, however, imagine these fragments to be only the chippings made by the masons in fitting the portcullises.

Beyond and below this vault is a second, somewhat smaller, in which General Vyse found an elegant sarcophagus of basalt : 'the outside was very beautifully carved in compartments in the Doric style,' or rather 'had the deep cornice which is characteristic of the Egyptian style.' It was empty, and the lid was found broken in the larger apartment. This valuable relic being very brittle, and in danger of disappearing under the curiosity of visitors, General Vyse removed the sarcophagus with great difficulty, and embarked it for England in 1838, but the vessel which conveyed it unfortunately went down off the coast of Spain.

The Red Pyramid was opened by the Moslems in the thirteenth century, when, the narrator states, 'nothing was found but the decayed rotten remains of a man, but there were no treasures, excepting some golden tablets, inscribed with characters which nobody could understand.' Some portion of the remains were found in the outer apartment, which are now deposited in the British Museum. Amongst them was the lid of a sarcophagus inscribed with an epitaph containing the king's name, which is at once identified with Mycerinus, to whom Herodotus attributes the erection of the pyramid.

Cartouche of Mycerinus.

At the eastern edge of the platform of Gizeh stands the Great Sphinx, a fabulous monster, compounded of the bust of a man with the body and legs of a lion. This combination is supposed to symbolise the union of intellect and power required in a king. The conception originated apparently in Thebes, and seems as intimately connected with that city as the pyramid is with Memphis. This gigantic monster is consequently some centuries later than the neighbouring Pyramids. Bunsen is inclined to assign it to Thothmes IV., who is represented, in a tablet on the breast of the Sphinx, offering incense and libations.

It is carved out of the living rock, excavated for the purpose to a depth of above sixty feet. The sands had so accumulated about the figure, that only the head, neck, and top of the back were visible, when Caviglia began to excavate the front in 1817. In recent years it has been wholly uncovered by M. Mariette. The figure lies with its face to the Nile, with the paws protruding, in an attitude of majestic repose. The countenance has the semi-negro, or ancient Egyptian cast of features, but is much injured by the Arabs hurling their spears and arrows at the ' idol.' Fragments of the beard have been found, and some traces of red remain on the cheeks, which are perhaps of a later date. The head was covered with a cap, of which, only the lower part remains. It is named in the hieroglyphics *Hor-em-Khoo*, ' Horus in the horizon ; ' that is to say, the Sun-god, the type of all the kings.

The height from the crown of the head to the floor between the paws

is seventy feet; the body is a hundred and forty feet in length, and the
paws protrude fifty feet more. Between them was the altar or temple where
sacrifices were offered to the deity, which was apparently the Genius of
the Theban monarchy. Rameses the Great is among the worshippers, and
inscriptions on the paws testify to the continuance of the rite in the
Roman age. A small building on the steps in front is inscribed to the
Emperor Severus, who visited Egypt A.D. 202.

From the floor, where the altar stood, a flight of forty-three steps as-
cended to a platform, whence an inclined plane led to the top of the rock
facing the Sphinx. The whole intermediate space had been excavated with
prodigious labour. Nothing could be grander than the appearance of this
mysterious creature fronting the worshippers, and rising more and more over
their heads, as they descended the long flight of steps to lay their offerings
at its feet.

The platform of Gizeh abounds in tombs of various ages, and more
than a hundred have been opened by Lepsius. One adorned with pillars,
and brilliantly painted, was the resting-place of a 'Prince Merhet,' a priest,
and, as Lepsius thinks 'more than probable,' a son, of Chufu; he is
described as 'superintendent of the royal buildings.' From these tombs the
enthusiastic explorer says—'I could almost write a court and state directory
of the time of King Cheops or Chephren.'¹ In another row of tombs Lepsius
imagines he has discovered the remains of the Fifth Dynasty, hitherto supposed to have reigned at Elephantine contemporaneously with the Fourth at
Memphis; but we must certainly hesitate to accept his conclusions, when he
tells us 'these are formed into one civilized epoch, dating about the year
4000 B.C.'¹ The common fault of Egyptologists is to assume a chronology
in their own minds, and then attach it to the monuments, as if it were
inscribed on them in unmistakable characters. Lepsius acknowledges that he
has 'not found a single cartouche that can be safely assigned to a period
previous to the Fourth Dynasty. The builders of the Great Pyramid seem
to assert their right to form the commencement of monumental history.'
The date of his 'civilized epoch,' therefore, will depend on that of the
Pyramids, which no sober chronology places higher than 2400 B.C., while
much may be said for a later date.

The ascent of the Great Pyramid is a rather laborious task. The great
blocks of stone form a series of steps of unequal height, varying from two
to four or five feet. A tribe of Arabs occupying a village at the foot claim
the right to assist travellers. Their sheikh levies a tribute of two shillings
upon each person making the ascent, and appoints two or three of his people
to help him up. The difficulty is thus materially diminished, and the magnificent view from the summit—even finer, in some respects, than that from
the Citadel—amply repays the traveller for the toil he has undergone. The

¹ *Letters*, iv.

ASCENDING THE GREAT PYRAMID.

desert stretches to the verge of the horizon. A narrow valley, inclosed by the Libyan and the Mokattam Mountains, runs to the southward. In the centre of this valley the noble river is seen winding along, with a belt of verdure on either side. The emerald green of the cultivated soil contrasts finely with the red of the mountains and the tawny sand of the desert. The pyramids of Sakkara, the palm groves of Mitrahenny, Cairo, with its innumerable minarets and cupolas, and the Citadel seated on its rocky height above the city, make up a picture which can scarcely be equalled, and which once seen can never be forgotten.

It is difficult, however, to abandon oneself to the full enjoyment of the scene. Crowds of Arabs follow the party to the summit, and pester them with entreaties for backsheesh, or with clamorous recommendations of the forged antiquities they have for sale. They are merry, good-humoured fellows, quick at taking a joke, and great as the annoyance may be, it is impossible to lose one's temper. I tried the effect of a retort upon them by asking backsheesh in return. One ragged scoundrel drew himself up with a dignified air, and putting his hand into some mysterious pocket of a cotton shirt, the only garment he possessed, drew out a small coin worth about half a farthing. Putting it into my hand with a condescending gesture, he folded his arms and walked away, amidst shouts of laughter from his comrades. To one of the dealers in forged antiquities, I said, ' I shan't buy those ; they were made in Birmingham.' A rival trader plucked me by the coat, and said, ' No, Mr. Doctor, his were not made in Birmingham ; his were made in London ; ' and then proceeded to vouch for his own as ' *bono anticos.*' One great feat is for an Arab to leap down the side of the First Pyramid, run across the intervening space of desert sand, and up the Second Pyramid in nine minutes. The sheikh was demanding a shilling apiece from the twenty-four Europeans who were on the summit. I remonstrated, saying that a dollar for the whole was the regular tariff. The sheikh drew me aside and whispered in my ear, ' Mr. Doctor, you say nothing, and pay nothing.' When he came round to collect the money from the contributors, he passed me by with a merry wink and shrug of his shoulders. A member of our party had a very powerful opera-glass, which he lent to one of the Arabs. Mohammed, looking through it, was beyond measure astounded to see not only his village in the plain below, but his two wives, Fatima and Zuleika, gaily disporting themselves in his absence, little thinking that ' he held them with his glittering eye.' When he had given free vent to his feelings, I said to him, ' Mohammed, how do you keep two wives in order ? We in England find one quite as much as we can manage with advantage ; sometimes rather more.' He replied, ' Oh, Mr. Doctor, dey berry good ; dey like two sisters ; I give them much stick ; ' and I have no doubt that they had a good deal of stick on his return home.

All this may seem quite out of keeping with the feelings proper to a visit to the Pyramids—as no doubt it is—but I have been so much annoyed by the unreality and sentimentalism of many books of travel, that I prefer to state facts exactly as they happened. The gift of a shilling to the sheikh, on condition that he allowed no one to speak to me for a quarter of an hour, at length secured a brief interval of quiet, in which I abandoned myself to the undisturbed enjoyment of the scene and its associations. What a wonderful history is unrolled before us as we look around! Across that waste of sand, which stretches away to the north-east, came Abram and Sarai his wife, and his nephew Lot, 'to sojourn in the land.' The young Hebrew slave, who should rise to be second only to Pharaoh, is brought by the same route, and is followed once and again by his brethren seeking corn in Egypt. Where the palm-trees cluster so thickly round the ruined mounds on the banks of the river, Moses and Aaron stood before the king, and demanded that he should let the people go. It was across the plain at our feet that the armies of Shishak and Pharaoh Necho marched for the invasion of Palestine. Here, too, came the fugitives, Jeroboam, Urijah, and others,[1] seeking refuge amongst their ancestral enemies. Near that obelisk of red granite rising amid the glossy green of the sugar-canes, Joseph married his wife : and when the Jewish monarchy had fallen, Onias, the high-priest, erected a temple upon the plan of that at Jerusalem for his brethren who had settled in Egypt. There, too, if we may trust tradition, the infant Saviour was brought when escaping from the wrath of 'Herod the king.' Turning from sacred to secular history, memories of Persian, Macedonian, and Roman conquerors — Cambyses, Alexander, and Cæsar—start into life as we look down upon the plain. Again the scene changes, as Amrou and Omar unfurl the banner of the False Prophet, and wrest the richest province of the empire from the enfeebled hand of the Byzantine rulers. Again, as we gaze, we seem to see at the head of his armies the magnificent Emir Yusef Salah-e'deen march from Cairo to confront the Crusaders under Richard the Lion-hearted, King of England, and, having given some of its most romantic chapters to modern history, to return, and dying, send his shroud round the city, whilst criers went before it, exclaiming, 'This is all that remains of the pomp of Saladin.' Coming down to our own times, we cannot forget the Battle of the Pyramids, when a small compact French army withstood the attack of 60,000 Mamlukes and compelled them to retreat, leaving 15,000 dead upon the field. In the four thousand years over which the history of Egypt extends, what generations have lived and died, what empires have risen and flourished and decayed! Surrounded by these affecting memorials of bygone ages, we seem to hear a voice sounding from the silence of the past, and saying, 'All flesh is grass, and all the goodliness thereof is as the flower of the field : the grass withereth, the flower fadeth : . . . but the word of our God shall stand for ever.'[2]

---

[1] 1 Kings xi. 40 ; xiv. 25, 26 ; Jeremiah xxvi. 21 ; xli. 17 ; xliii. 7.   [2] Isaiah xl. 6, 8.

CAIRO TO ASSOUAN.

MONEY-CHANGER AT SIOUT.

ON THE BANKS OF THE NILE.

SECTION II.

CAIRO TO ASSOUAN.

' CAIRO to Assiût direct by railway!' Grotesque as this sounds, it has for some years been possible, a railway having been constructed over the 230 miles separating the two towns. Few persons, however, would care to 'do' the Nile in this fashion.

The traveller, who wishes really to enjoy the journey, has the choice of two preferable modes of transit. He may go by steamer or by dahabiyyeh. If pressed for time and of limited purse, he must needs choose the former. If he is able to control abundant supply of money and time, he may choose the latter. Since 1870 the steamer arrangements on the Nile have been passing more and more completely under the control of Messrs. T. Cook & Son. This firm has now almost a monopoly of the steamer traffic on the Nile. The result is that a regular service of boats runs between Cairo and the First

Cataract twice weekly during the season, from November to March. New steamers, constructed with a knowledge of all the special requirements of the service, have begun running this year (1886); and what used to be both a formidable and costly journey, is now within the reach of all who can afford to visit the East. Travellers who make the journey by dahabiyyeh often find that the smoothness and enjoyment of the trips are increased by leaving the needful arrangements in the hands of the same firm.

CREW OF NILE BOAT.

The chief advantage of the steamboat trip is that we are able to run rapidly past the uninteresting portions of the river. The Nile scenery is for the most part dull and flat. On a dahabiyyeh we may find ourselves becalmed for days off a mud-bank or a long stretch of sand, with nothing to do except watching the antics or listening to the monotonous singing of the crew. If, weary of waiting for a wind, the crew are ordered to tow the boat against the stream, the progress is exceedingly slow and tedious—six or eight miles a day are the utmost that can be accomplished.

But steamboat speed is not secured without great compensating disadvantages. The delicious sense of repose, the Oriental *Kief*, the Italian *dolce far niente*, which constitutes so large a part of the enjoyment of the Nile trip, is impossible on board a steamer. Though the rate of progress be slow as compared with that on European or American waters, it is yet far too rapid to let us abandon ourselves to the lotus-eating indolence which is so refreshing to the wearied frame and over-wrought brain of the traveller in search of health. Then, too, it is impossible to linger where we please. We must hurry on. Two hours may be enough for the tombs of Beni Hassan, three hours for the temple of Esneh, four days for Luxor and Karnak; but it is distressing to feel that we cannot stop if we like. Haunted by the fear of being too late, we complete our survey, watch in

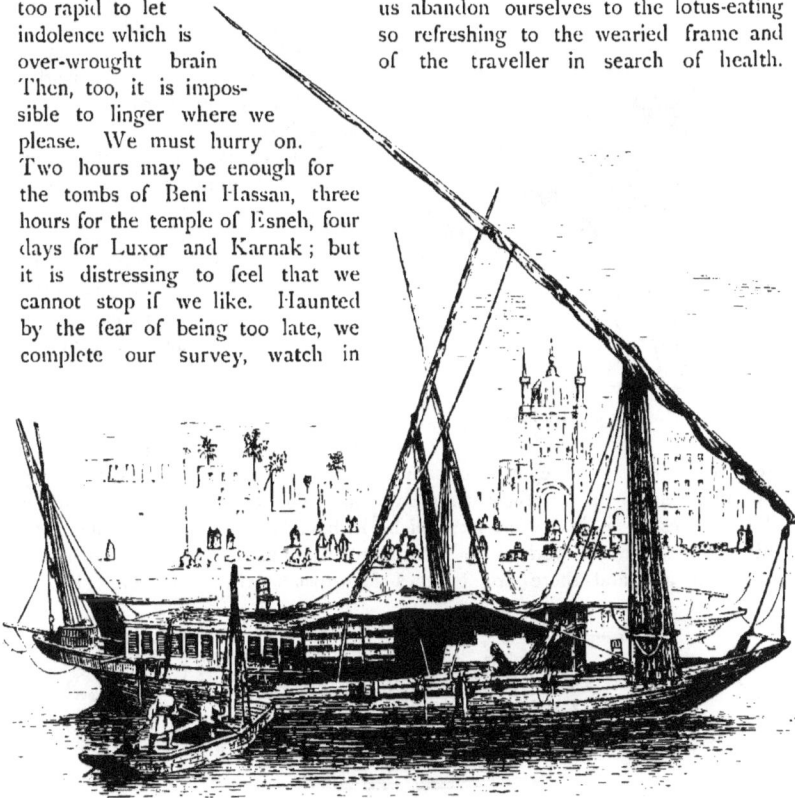

A DAHABIYYEH OR NILE BOAT.

hand, to be sure of catching the steamer before she leaves her moorings in the river. The risk of finding uncongenial company on board is likewise not inconsiderable. In a public conveyance it is not possible to choose one's fellow-travellers, and it may happen that our meditations on the grand memories of the past are being perpetually broken in upon by 'men whose talk is of bullocks.' A very serious objection to the old steamers used to be their scandalously dirty condition, and the swarms of vermin with which they were infested. This, of course, does not now apply; the new vessels being as clean and as comfortable as the most fastidious can desire. Nevertheless, for those who have ample means and leisure, and who have resources within themselves, or in their party, to bear the monotony of some days or weeks on board a boat with nothing to do and little to see, the Nile trip in a dahabiyyeh is one of the most delightful excursions in the world. To others the steamer offers a very fair substitute.

But what is a dahabiyyeh? The dahabiyyeh, gentle reader, is a boat in form and outline not unlike the barges of the City Companies in the days when the Thames was to Londoners what the Nile is to the Egyptians. Its saloons and cabins are on deck. Some are luxuriously fitted up, room being found even for a piano. They differ in size, affording accommodation for from two to six or eight passengers.

KITCHEN OF NILE BOAT.

For the crew no sleeping accommodation whatever is provided. They roll themselves up in their *burnouses* and lie down on the fore-deck like bundles of old clothes, for which I have not infrequently mistaken them. The boat is worked by two large triangular sails fitted to masts fore and aft, and there are benches for rowers when needed. The re-

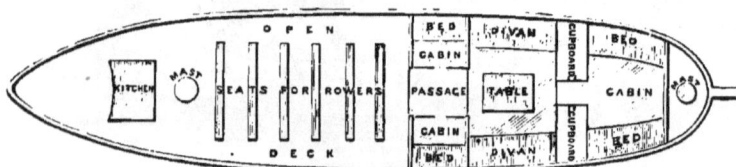

PLAN OF DAHABIYYEH, FOR FOUR PERSONS, SIXTY FEET LONG.

semblance between the Nile boats of the present day and those of the ancient Egyptians, as depicted on the monuments, has been often noticed. 'Joseph, in the flush of power, probably journeyed thus through Egypt, only, of course, with a royal magnificence and splendour of appointment to be dreamed of rather than described. All the travel of those days between the upper and lower country, the traffic of Thebes and Memphis, would be done in such vessels. It must be remembered, that, although Egypt is nearly eight hundred miles in length, its average breadth is only ten or twelve, of which the river is the great feature, the centre and source of fertility and wealth. Thus every city was by the water side. Egypt was emphatically "a place of broad rivers and streams," white, in those palmy days, with the swelling sail of many a gallant ship, and populous with galleys. So conservative, too, in its customs was it, that even the

DHOW OR TRADING BOAT ON THE NILE.

Ptolemies and Romans were forced to follow them. Thus perhaps Cleopatra's famous barge may have been but a gorgeous dahabiyyeh :

> The barge she sat in, like a burnished throne,
> Burned on the water, the poop was beaten gold.
> Purple the sails, and so perfumèd that
> The winds were love-sick with them : the oars were silver,
> Which to the tune of flutes kept stroke.'

Dahabiyyehs run up the river without stopping, except when becalmed or to lie-to for the night. Places of interest are visited on the return to Cairo. It will, however, suit our convenience better to take them in reverse order.

Our first halting-place will be Bedresheyn, fifteen miles from Bûlâk, to visit the site of ancient Memphis and the Pyramids of Sakkâra. There is a

curious Mussulman tradition in connection with this village, from which its
name is said to have been derived. The orthodox creed of Islam is that
women will be saved like men, and will be made young again on entering
heaven. This legend, however, affirms that there is one exception to the
rule. Joseph, when Grand Vizier of Egypt, was riding out from Memphis,
when an aged woman accosted him and implored alms. So wrinkled and
deformed was she, that he could not help exclaiming, ' How ugly thou
art!' ' Pray, then, to Allah,' she replied, ' that he would make me young
and beautiful. He hears all thy prayers, and grants whatever thou dost

PROSTRATE COLOSSAL STATUE OF RAMESES II. AT MEMPHIS.

ask.' Thereupon Joseph lifted up his hands and prayed for her as she
requested. Instantly she stood by his side transformed into a lovely girl—
so lovely that he was enamoured of her and made her his wife. She lived
long, and survived him for many years. Dying in extreme old age, she went
to heaven, an old woman, the only old woman there : for Allah makes all
good women young again once, but once only, and she can never be made
young again.

The road from the village leads through one of the most luxuriant
palm forests to be found in Egypt. Our boat was moored for the night
close to the point where an avenue of trees came down to the river-bank.

The full moon was shining with wonderful brilliancy, pouring a flood of light over the landscape, of which we, in these northern latitudes, can form little conception. I went ashore and wandered for hours among the tall columnar stems and under the graceful feathery crowns of the palm-trees. A party of villagers, too astonished even to ask for backsheesh, came out to gaze at the strange sight of a European wandering about after nightfall. On my expressing a wish for some of the fronds which hung overhead, a lithe, agile fellow clambered up like a monkey and plucked half-a-dozen for me. Among the many pleasant memories which I brought back from Egypt, there are none more pleasant than that of the moonlight walk through the palm groves of Mitrahenny.

There are few remains above ground of the splendour of ancient Memphis. The city has utterly disappeared. If any traces of it yet exist, they are buried beneath the vast mounds of crumbling bricks and broken pottery which meet the eye in every direction. Near the village of Mitrahenny is a colossal statue of Rameses the Great. It is apparently one of two described by Herodotus and Diodorus as standing in front of the Temple of Ptah. They were originally about fifty feet in height. The one which remains, though mutilated, measures forty-eight feet. It is finely carved in a limestone which takes a high polish, and is evidently a portrait. It lies in a pit, which during the inundation is filled with water. As we gaze at this fallen and battered statue of the mighty conqueror, who was probably contemporaneous with Moses, it is impossible not to remember the words of the prophet Isaiah :—' They

RAMESES II.

that see thee shall narrowly look upon thee, and consider thee, saying, Is this the man that made the earth to tremble, that did shake kingdoms ; that made the world as a wilderness, and destroyed the cities thereof; that opened not the house of his prisoners ? All the kings of the nations, even all of them, lie in glory, every one in his own house. But thou art cast out of thy grave like an abominable branch, and as the raiment of those that are slain, thrust through with a sword, that go down to the stones of the pit.' '

Riding across the mounds of débris already referred to, we soon reach

' Isaiah xiv. 16-19.

the vast subterranean tomb in which, for a period of at least fifteen hundred years, the bodies of the sacred bulls were interred. In the year 1856, M. Mariette observed the head of a sphinx protruding from the sand, and remembered that Strabo described the Serapeum of Memphis as approached

SARCOPHAGUS IN THE SERAPEUM OF MEMPHIS.

through an avenue of sphinxes. He at once commenced his explorations in search of the temple in which Apis was worshipped when alive, and the tomb in which it was buried when dead. With immense exertions, the sand-drift was cleared away, and the avenue was laid bare from beneath a superincumbent mass, which was in some places seventy feet in depth. The splendour of this imposing approach may be inferred from the fact that one hundred and forty-one sphinxes were discovered *in situ*, besides the pedestals of many others. The temple to which they led has disappeared, but the tomb remains. It consists of a huge vault or tunnel, divided into three parts, one of which was four hundred yards in length, another two hundred and ten yards. Only the latter of these is now accessible. Chambers lead out from it on either side, in each of which is a ponderous granite sarcophagus hollowed out in the centre. In this cavity, which will hold four or five persons with ease, the embalmed body of the sacred bull was deposited. A granite slab of great size and weight, placed over the sarcophagus, closed it like a lid. The Viceroy, anxious to place one of these sarcophagi in his museum at Bûlâk, succeeded in conveying it from the chamber into the subterranean passage. But there it remains. The inclined plane which leads to the surface of the soil offers an insurmountable obstacle to its further progress. Yet the ancient Egyptians transported these huge blocks of granite from the quarries near Syene to Memphis, a distance of nearly six hundred miles!

The pomp and splendour with which the worship of the bull Apis was celebrated at Memphis may help us to understand the apostasy of the Israelites in the wilderness, when, having made a molten calf, they said, 'These be thy gods, O Israel, which brought thee up out of the land of Egypt.'[1] They had been so accustomed to see divine honours paid, even by the mightiest of their task-masters, to this supposed incarnation of the Deity, that at Sinai itself they yielded to the influence of long habit, and 'corrupted themselves, turning aside quickly out of the way which the Lord commanded them.'

It was not the bull alone which was worshipped during life by the Egyptians and embalmed on its death. Every nome, almost every city, had its tutelar animal, which received similar honours. Dogs, cats, jackals, wolves, crocodiles, baboons, held in abhorrence in one district, were revered in another. Thus the Tentyrites, regarding the crocodile as the symbol of Typhon, killed it as a religious duty. Elsewhere, temples were built in its honour, in which these disgusting reptiles were tended with the most sedulous care. In all parts of Egypt are large pits, in which the embalmed remains of various animals are to be found in prodigious numbers. One species of ibis seems to have been worshipped everywhere. The bird itself has disappeared, but its embalmed remains exist by millions. Bayle St. John, who made his way into the Ibis pits near Memphis, says: 'We began to explore a vast succession of galleries and apartments, closed up here and there with walls of unburnt brick. I can give no idea of the extent of these bird catacombs, except by saying that they appeared large enough to contain all

---

[1] Exodus xxxii. 4, 8.

the defunct members of the feathered creation since the beginning of the world. Some of the chambers were vast caves, and there were hundreds of them.' It was scarcely an exaggeration of the Roman satirist, who, when

THE IBIS.

ridiculing the animal worship of the Egyptians, said that it was 'more easy in Egypt to find a god than a man.'

In the sandy plains near the site of Memphis are the Pyramids of

Sakkâra. They stand in a vast necropolis four and a half miles in length, where lie interred the dead of the earliest periods of Egyptian history. One of them is built in stages, and is said by a doubtful tradition preserved by Manetho to have been erected by a monarch of the First Dynasty. If this be true, it is much older than those of Gizeh, and is the most ancient monument in the world. The Gizeh Pyramids, from their superior size and imposing position, have come to be spoken of as *the Pyramids*, leading many persons to suppose that they are the only ones. This, however, is a mistake. There are eleven still standing in Sakkâra. Throwing out of account various pyramidal structures in Upper Egypt, Ethiopia, and elsewhere, the total number may be put down at about a hundred. They are not scattered indiscriminately throughout the country, but occupy an area about forty-five miles in length, from Gizeh in the north to the Fâyûm in the

IBIS MUMMY FROM MEMPHIS.

south. Some persons have conjectured that their concentration within these limits seems to point to some peculiar phase of religion or civilisation as prevailing at the period of their erection, and that they were built, not by a native Egyptian race, but by foreign conquerors, who had placed their capital at Memphis, and introduced this mode of sepulchre, which lasted only during their period of occupation, and ceased when they were expelled. This view has not found favour with Egyptologists, and there can be no doubt that they were pyramid-sepulchres.

We cannot leave the plain of Memphis without recurring yet once again to the most memorable event in all its eventful history. It was probably here that Moses and Aaron stood before Pharaoh and demanded that he should let the people go. In the city now buried beneath mouldering heaps and desert sand the faithful and fearless leader braved the 'wrath of the king: for he endured, as seeing Him who is invisible.' This was the spot where 'Pharaoh rose up in the night, he, and all his servants, and all the Egyptians; and there was a great cry in Egypt; for there was not a house where there was not one dead.'[1] Our thoughts pass away from the palaces smitten with this sudden and sore bereavement to the homes of the enslaved race waiting securely for the signal to depart, whilst through faith they 'kept the passover, and the sprinkling of blood, lest He that destroyed the first-born should touch them.'[2] Great as was the historical importance of this event, seeing that it was the birth of a nation, it gains yet deeper significance in the fact that it was a type of the great Antitype: 'For even Christ our passover is sacrificed for us.'[3]

It is of the next one hundred and fifty or two hundred miles of the journey up the Nile that travellers often complain as being tedious and wearisome. The scenery is monotonous, and the monumental remains are few and unimportant. And yet I cannot say that I felt either tedium or weariness. The great river itself is a constant source of wonder. For fifteen hundred miles below the point at which the Tacazze enters it from the mountains of Abyssinia, it flows onward to the sea without receiving a single tributary. Not even a tiny rill or brooklet trickles through the desert sand throughout this immense distance, and rain is almost unknown. The main occupation of the peasantry on its banks is to pump water from its ample stream. Sâkiyehs and shâdûfs are busy all day and all night long levying contributions upon it for the irrigation of the land. Absorbed throughout its course by the scorching sand, and evaporated by an unclouded sun, its volume remains apparently undiminished. Fed by the lakes, and annually swollen by the tropical rains of Central Africa, it is an object of ceaseless interest.

Then the atmospheric phenomena are of great variety and beauty. There is, indeed, no 'weather' on the Nile, in our English sense of the term. By force of habit we commence the voyage by saying, 'Fine morning;' 'Fine evening;' but gradually we awake to the consciousness that every day is fine. The subtle criticisms, the striking and original remarks on the weather, which make up so large a part of the small talk of con-versation at home, are felt to be absurdly out of place where rain is almost a prodigy. In the early spring the *khamsîn* does, indeed, afford a very unpleasant change to comment upon. It is a hot, dry wind, laden with fine particles of dust, which penetrate everywhere, fill one's eyes and ears, irritate the skin, and produce a sense of extreme discomfort. Everything is seen through a lurid haze. The sands of the desert are whirled by it into rotating columns, which march to and fro till they suddenly break up and disappear. On the river this is merely a cause of annoyance, but in the

<hr/>

[1] Exodus xii. 30.   [2] Hebrews xi. 28.   [3] 1 Corinthians v. 7.

SAND-STORM IN THE DESERT.

desert it becomes a serious danger. Caravans are said to have perished and been buried beneath the drifting sands. Apart from this most undesirable 'change in the weather,' the days resemble one another. But

MAP OF THE NILE, FROM ALEXANDRIA TO THE SECOND CATARACT.

the parts of each day have to the observant eye an ever-varying charm. The mornings are delightful, clear and cool and bright, with no mist to blur the outlines or veil the sun. Towards mid-day, all colour seems to be discharged from the landscape, which is wrapped in a white, blinding glare.

G

Yet even now it is pleasant to lie under an awning on deck, and with a feeling of delicious indolence listen to the lapping of the water against the sides of the boat, and watch the banks glide past us as in a dream. With the drawing on of evening a glory of colour comes out in the light of the setting sun. Purple shadows are cast by the mountains. The reds and greys of sandstone, granite, and limestone cliffs blend exquisitely with the tawny yellow of the desert, the rich green of the banks and the blue of the river, giving combinations and contrasts of colour in which the artist revels. The cold grey twilight follows immediately upon sunset; but in a few minutes there is a marvellous change. The earth and sky are suffused with a delicate pink tinge, known as the after-glow. This is the most fairy-like and magical

NILE CLIFFS.

effect of colour I have ever seen. Swiss travellers are familiar with something like it in the rosy flush of the snowy Alps before sunrise and after sunset. The peculiarity in Egypt is that light and colour return after an interval of ashy grey, like the coming back of life to a corpse, and that it is not confined to a part of the landscape, but floods the whole. I have seen no explanation of this most beautiful phenomenon, and can only conjecture that it is connected with the reflection and refraction of the light of the setting sun from the sands of the Libyan Desert. Then comes on the night—and such a night! The stars shine with a lustrous brilliancy so intense that I have seen a distinct shadow cast by the planet Jupiter, whilst his satellites were easily visible through an ordinary opera-glass.[1] Orion was an object of indescribable splendour. Under which of her aspects the moon was most beautiful I cannot say—whether the first slender thread of light, invisible in our denser atmosphere, or in her growing brightness, or in her full-orbed radiance. Addison's familiar lines gained a new meaning when read under this hemisphere of glory :

Soon as the evening shades prevail,
The moon takes up the wondrous tale,
And, nightly, to the listening earth,
Repeats the story of her birth ;
Whilst all the stars that round her burn,
And all the planets in their turn,
Confirm the tidings as they roll,
And spread the truth from pole to pole.

AN EGYPTIAN VILLAGE.

The river flows on through a narrow strip of vegetation varying from a few feet to a few miles in width, but always bounded by the desert. Sometimes the mountains retreat to a considerable distance from the river, sometimes they come down to its very brink, and form a series of bold cliffs, often surmounted by a Coptic convent. The villages are commonly picturesque, as seen from a distance, standing as they do under a grove of palms, and often placed on the top of a mound which hides the ruins of an ancient city. But on a nearer approach they are dirty and dilapidated beyond description. Still these wretched squalid hamlets have a charm for the European traveller.

[1] On one occasion we believed that we could see the principal satellite with the naked eye. Is this possible?

The minaret of the mosque, though often constructed only of mud, is brilliant with white-wash, and it rises gracefully amongst the palm-trees. At sunset, after nightfall, at daybreak, at noon, and towards evening, the Muezzin takes his stand in the gallery, and in a loud, sonorous voice calls the faithful to prayer — 'God is most great. I testify that there is no Deity but God. I testify that Mohammed is God's apostle. Come to prayer. Come to security. God is most great;' adding, during the night, and in the early morning, 'Prayer is better than sleep.' Attached to the mosque is commonly a school, the noise of which is a sufficient guide to the spot. The children recite their lessons all together, and each scholar endeavours to make his voice heard above the din by shouting his loudest. The instruction given is of the slightest possible kind, consisting of little else than the recitation of the

THE CALL TO PRAYER.

Korán and the simplest rules of arithmetic. The master is often a blind man, who, being able to repeat the Korán by rote, can teach it to the children. His payment is little more than nominal, but is apparently quite equal to his merits. Mr. Lane gives some curious illustrations of the nature of the instruction given, and tells the following droll story: 'I was lately told of a man who could neither read nor write succeeding to the office

THE SCHOOL OF SULTAN HASSAN.
(After F. Goodall, R.A.)

of a schoolmaster in my neighbourhood. Being able to recite the whole of the Korán, he could hear the boys repeat their lessons : to write them, he employed the "'areef" (or head boy and monitor in the school), pretending that his eyes were weak. A few days after he had taken upon himself this office, a poor woman brought a letter for him to read to her from her son, who had gone on pilgrimage. The fikee pretended to read it, but said nothing ; and the woman, inferring from his silence that the letter contained bad news, said to him :—"Shall I shriek ?" He answered "Yes." "Shall I tear my clothes?" she asked. He replied, "Yes." So the poor woman returned to her house, and with her assembled friends performed the lamentation and other ceremonies usual on the occasion of a death. Not many days after this, her son arrived, and she asked him what he could mean by causing a letter to be written stating that he was dead. He explained the contents of the letter, and she went to the schoolmaster and begged him to inform her why he had told her to shriek, and to tear her clothes, since the letter was to inform her that her son was well, and he was now arrived at home. Not at all abashed, he said, "God knows futurity. How could I know that your son would arrive in safety? It was better that you should think him dead than be led to expect to see him, and perhaps be disappointed." Some persons who were sitting with him praised his wisdom, exclaiming, "Truly our new fikee is a man of unusual judgment," and for a little while he found that he had raised his reputation by this blunder.'

EGYPTIAN FOWLER.
(*From the British Museum.*)

The profusion of bird-life on the Nile is one of its most striking features. Myriads of storks, cranes, geese, wild ducks, pelicans, hawks, pigeons, and herons are seen clustering on the islands in the river, lining its banks, or flying in dense clouds overhead. To protect the growing crops the fellaheen often construct little stands for boys armed with slings, who acquire wonderful dexterity in bringing down their feathered game. In Ancient Egypt birds were as numerous as now. Geese are represented as forming an important part of every banquet, and they are seldom wanting in the offerings to the gods. Fowling was a favourite amusement. Visitors to the British Museum are familiar with the tablet which represents the flocks of geese possessed by a large landed proprietor. In another the sportsman is seen catching water-fowl in a thicket of papyrus and lotus-lilies on the river-bank; a decoy duck stands on the prow of his boat, and a cat is trained to act as a retriever.[1] These countless flocks of birds may serve to illustrate the dream of Pharaoh's chief baker. 'I had three white baskets on my head: and in the uppermost basket there was of all manner of bakemeats for Pharaoh; and the birds did eat them out of the basket upon my head.'[2]

Quadrupeds are much less numerous. As in all Oriental countries, homeless, masterless dogs roam round the villages, and act as scavengers. Among the swamps of the Delta wild boars are

WATCHING FIELDS IN EGYPT.

---

[1] An English nobleman who visited the Nile for purposes of sport published, on his return, an account of his prowess. He shot, within two months, 9 pelicans; 1514 geese; 328 wild ducks; 47 widgeon; 5 teal; 66 pintails; 47 flamingoes (!); 37 curlews; 112 herons; 2 quails; 9 partridges; 3,283 pigeons; and 117 miscellaneous. Total, 5,576 head. Even persons who are not scrupulous in the matter must concur in reprobating this wholesale and useless slaughter.   [2] Genesis xl. 16, 17.

common. Jackals and foxes may be met with everywhere. In the neighbourhood of Luxor and Karnak a hyæna is often seen, with its heavy, clumsy form and slouching gait, prowling amongst the ruins. The crocodile has almost disappeared from Lower Egypt. Notwithstanding its impenetrable coat of mail and its terrible jaws, it is a shy, timid creature, and is said to have been driven away by the paddle-wheels of the steamboats. Formerly they might occasionally be seen sunning themselves on the mud and sandbanks between Kench and Assouan, but they have not been seen between these points now for a number of years past. It is only as we enter Nubia that they are found in considerable numbers.

The flora of Egypt is not very remarkable. Excepting palms, the trees are few and unimportant. A few fine sycamores may be seen, generally in the neighbourhood of a mosque, or shadowing a *santon's* tomb. Midway between Cairo and the First Cataract the Doum palm makes its appearance. It differs greatly from the ordinary date-palm. Instead of the single straight stem, it divides into two main branches, which again bifurcate as the tree grows. Its fruit, which is about the size and colour of a pomegranate, is said to taste like gingerbread. It contains an exceedingly hard stone, which is used by the modern, as it was by the ancient, Egyptian carpenters for making sockets, drills, and hinges.

One very remarkable change has passed upon the water-plants of the Nile. The lotus and the papyrus were formerly the most common and characteristic of its products, insomuch that they formed the symbols of Upper and Lower Egypt. The papyrus was used not only for making paper, to which it gave its name, but for the construction of boats, baskets, and innumerable other

THE PAPYRUS PLANT.

articles; as in the Upper Jordan Valley, where it still grows abundantly, even cottages were built with it. No religious service, no state ceremonial, no domestic festival is found without the lotus flower. It forms part of every offering to the gods. The guests at a banquet all hold one in their hands. It is, perhaps, the object of all others most constantly represented on the monuments. Yet both the lotus and the papyrus have disappeared from Egypt. No trace of either can be found.[1] Unaccountable as is the disappearance of these plants, it was yet foretold by the prophet Isaiah, as a part of the Divine judgment upon Egypt: 'The brooks of defence shall be emptied and dried up : the reeds and flags shall wither. The paper reeds by the brooks, . and everything sown by the brooks, shall wither, be

EGYPTIAN ENTERTAINMENT; EACH GUEST WITH A LOTUS FLOWER.
(From the British Museum.)

driven away, and be no more.'[2] The phrase 'brooks of defence' in this passage has greatly perplexed commentators. Brooks, in the proper sense of the term, there are none in Egypt. Of course the reference is to the canals with which the country is intersected. But why 'brooks of defence'? It has been commonly supposed that they were constructed simply for irrigation. But it affords a striking illustration of the minute accuracy of Scripture phraseology to find that they served the further purpose of guarding the land against the raids of the Bedouin horsemen, who then,

---

[1] It is indeed said that, in some remote and unvisited portions of the Delta, an occasional papyrus reed may be discovered. The fact is doubted, and the statement in the text is substantially true.

[2] Isaiah xix. 6, 7.

as now, infested the desert, and whose depredations were checked by these canals.

There is little to interest or detain us in the modern towns on the Nile bank. Occasionally, as at Manfalût, the governor's palace offers some characteristic bits of Arabic architecture. These, however, are rare. Even in the larger towns, Kench, for instance, or Siût, there is little to be seen save wretched, dilapidated hovels, lanes almost impassable for their filth and narrowness, with, here and there, a huge sugar factory or cotton mill worked by forced labour for the benefit of the Viceroy. The situation of Siût (Assiût, as it is now usually spelt) is very beautiful. A ride of about two miles over a raised causeway, which leads amongst fields of great fertility, brings us to a picturesque gateway not unlike that at Manfalût. In front of it is a large courtyard, overshadowed by fine trees, in which are seated numbers of fellaheen or townspeople waiting to present petitions to the governor, or to plead their cause before him. In one corner a group of conscripts are squatting, who have been dragged from their homes to serve in the army, the navy, or the factories of the Khedive, as the officials may decide. Entering the city gate, we find ourselves in the capital of Upper Egypt. The bazaars, though dark and gloomy, are crowded with buyers and sellers. A military officer, peacefully mounted on a donkey, is transacting business at the door of a money-changer's shop. A group of Bedouin are bargaining

LOTUS FLOWER AND LEAF.
(*Nymphæa Lotus.*)

for swords, daggers, and long Arab guns at an armourer's forge. Veiled women are haggling over the price of a piece of blue cloth or a measure of flour. Passing out from this busy scene by the gate on the opposite side of the city to that at which we entered, we find ourselves almost immediately in the silence and solitude of the great Libyan Desert. Fragments of mummies, mummy-cases, and cere-cloth lie about unheeded on the sand. The steep, rocky hill-side is honeycombed with tombs, in which are found remains of embalmed wolves. It was from the worship of these animals that the town took its ancient name of Lycopolis. The view from the

MANFALÛT.

summit of this range of hills is very striking, especially as I saw it, at sunset. Except where the Valley of the Nile broke the monotony, the eye ranged over a boundless expanse of desert. To the very verge of the horizon stretched undulations of marl and sand, like the long swell of ocean in a calm. On the edge of the cultivated soil a few black tents of the Bedouin were pitched. Two or three Arabs, their naked bodies almost black with exposure, were stalking solemnly across the silent waste at our feet, over which long shadows were cast in the slanting beams of the setting sun. They were laden with the skins of wild beasts, which they were bringing into Siût to sell. No other living beings were visible, and they harmonised well with the sentiment of the scene. I felt at the time that the grandest mountain scenery of Switzerland was less impressive than this sublime monotony of sky and desert.

It is but seldom that ordinary travellers can have any direct communication with the people of the country. The language in most cases forms an insuperable barrier. The fellah can speak nothing but Arabic, of which the traveller is commonly quite ignorant. If the dragoman is employed as interpreter, he is pretty sure to reproduce the comical scene described by Kinglake.[1] The donkey-boys and local guides often know a little English, of which they make very droll use. I was greatly amused and puzzled by the application of the word *lunch*. 'See,

GOVERNOR'S PALACE AT MANFALÛT.

Osiris hab lunch,' said my guide one day, pointing to an altar piled with offering before the god, sculptured on a temple wall. On another occasion, riding through some fields of *doorah* and vetch, I was told that the former was 'Arabs' lunch;' the latter, 'camels' lunch.' The explanation I found to be, that as Europeans breakfast and dine on board their boat, whilst lunch is often eaten on shore, it is the only meal of which the natives see or hear anything; hence it has come to be used for food in general.

[1] *Eothen*, vol. i. p. 12.

Whenever travellers can speak or read to the people in their own language, they are listened to with eager interest. Readers of the *Sunday at Home* are familiar with Miss Whately's interesting narratives of conversations with them. Having described the songs and rude music of the boat's crew, she says :—

'At last, after several songs and dances, the whole party became tired, and began to light their pipes. It seemed a sad thing that these poor fellows should have nothing better than such childish diversions ere they went to rest. After a little consultation, it was agreed to desire our Moslem servant to ask if they would like the lady to read them a story. "What! in Arabic? Could the Sitt (*lady*) read Arabic?" they asked, incredulously, not knowing that the lady in question was from Syria, and Arabic her native tongue. They all said it was good, and they would like to listen.

'So the Arabic Bible was brought out, and, muffled in our cloaks, we sat on the deck beside our friend, who was seated on a box; one of us held a *fanous*, or native lamp, which threw its bright light on the sacred page, while all around was darkness, except where the moon here and there shone on the swarthy faces of the Nubian boatmen, who formed a circle about us, crouching in various postures, and wrapped in their striped blue and crimson mantles. The servants stood leaning against the masts, listening with deep attention; not a sound interrupted the reader's voice but the low ripple of the current, as the water plashed against the sides of the boat. It was a scene one would never forget—that first opening of God's book in the presence of these ignorant, benighted followers of the False Prophet. Our friend read of the sheep lost in the wilderness, and the piece of silver lost in the house—those simple illustrations of God's wondrous dealings with man, which are understood and felt in every age and every land. Then she read the history of the prodigal son, and the interest of the hearers increased, and was shown by their frequent exclamations of "Good!"—"Praise God!" —"That is wonderful!"—"Ha!"'(with an expressive tone impossible to write, though easy to conceive). The look of intelligence which the silvery rays of the moon revealed on more than one dark upturned face and bright black eyes spoke no less plainly.

'As she went on, pausing occasionally to explain a word or show the application, it was deeply interesting to watch the effect on her listeners; and when she closed the book, fearing to tire them, there was a universal cry of "Lissa! lissa!" (Not yet! not yet!) She read then the Ten Commandments, pointing out the necessity for atonement, as shown by man's frequent breaking of God's laws.

'One of the men made a remark relative to the inferiority of women, whom he affirmed, according to Moslem doctrine, to be not only weaker, but more sinful creatures than man. He did not intend anything personal by this, for the Sitt was evidently looked on as one quite beyond the common race of women ; and we heard them observe to each other, with most emphatic gestures, that she was " very good ! " and " knew everything ! " Without manifesting surprise or annoyance, she explained to him the love of God for all His creatures, and the equal necessity for His pardon for all.

'" If the water in a vessel is pure," she said, "it signifies but little what the vessel is in itself, whether of clay or of silver; and the Spirit of God, dwelling in our hearts, can alone make us vessels fit for the Master's use ; whatever we are by nature. He will give us His Holy Spirit, and change our sinful hearts, if we ask as He has told us."'

The boatmen's songs referred to by Miss Whately are amongst the most familiar memories of a Nile trip. The crew, whether rowing or hauling on a rope, or squatting in a circle on the deck with nothing to do, will continue hour after hour intoning a monotonous and interminable chant, the words of which are frequently quite unmeaning. The principal performer improvises a single line, to which his companions add a chorus, and, when possible, mark the time by a rhythmical clapping of hands, and the measured beat of a *tarabookah*. The following is a fair specimen :

'I wish I was at Osioot,	O Allah ! O my prophet !
O Allah ! O my prophet !	The wind is blowing very strong,
Then I'd buy a new felt cap,	O Allah ! O my prophet !' etc., etc.

Mr. Macgregor, in his amusing and interesting little book, *Eastern Music*, has given some of these chants, which he caught by ear and noted down. Here is one :

Con spirito.

A - dy joob - ta sa - li - a - ra ka - la - fo, A - dy joob - ta sa - li - a - ra ka - la - fo, Mi - ny och - tin an - i - o - kit a - - ka - dy buk - ke - ty a - ni poy - no.

He gives another, a great favourite on the Nile. We are told that it was played 'With the Nile drum obligato, and a clapping of hands at every bar.' The Egyptian drum is called *tarabookah*, and that used by the Nile boatmen is generally made of clay covered with fishes' skin. It is placed under the left arm, generally suspended by a string that passes over the left shoulder, and is beaten with both hands. It yields different sounds when struck near the edge and in the middle. The mode of accompanying a song by clapping the hands is very ancient, and may be seen depicted in several engravings in Wilkinson's *Manners and Customs of the Ancient Egyptians*. We quote the first eight bars because the melody is remarkable for the introduction of the minor seventh (the F natural) in the sixth bar, which gives it a peculiar effect, and is an evidence of its extreme antiquity.

LOVE SONG OF THE NILE BOATMEN.

Allegro.

Am re - val in o - lo moo   Hub - by a - mo re - val at - sin

Fren me no a ra ba   Hub - by a ko re mo se lat.   etc.

From the natural scenery and modern life of Egypt, we return to the monumental remains of the Pharaohs and the Ptolemies.

At various points along the banks of the river we may observe lines of chambers cut into the face of the cliffs. Originally tombs, they were, after the introduction of Christianity, used as cells by hermits and anchorites. The most interesting of them are at Beni Hassan, about one hundred and sixty miles above Cairo. They form a terrace, approached by the remains of an ancient causeway, which rises from the plain and runs along the front of the grottoes. The rock has been hewn out into architraves and columns, with doorways leading into the tombs. They thus have the appearance of buildings rather than caverns. The columns are remarkable for their non-Egyptian character. If found elsewhere, they would be at once classed as Doric, yet they belong to the earliest period of the Egyptian monarchy, and are probably but little later than the era of the Pyramids. No Greek

PORTICO OF THE TOMB OF THE NOMARK ANENI AT BENI HASSAN.

influence can therefore be suspected. The walls of the chambers are covered with frescoes representing the every-day life of the time. Men and women are wrestling, fishing and ploughing, reaping, trapping birds, giving dinner-parties, being flogged, *cutting their toe-nails*, treading the winepress, dancing, playing the harp, weaving linen, playing at ball, being shaved by the barber, playing at draughts. Verily, there is nothing new under the sun! Life in Egypt four thousand years ago was almost identical with that of England in the present day. One of my companions was a Cumberland squire, and

H

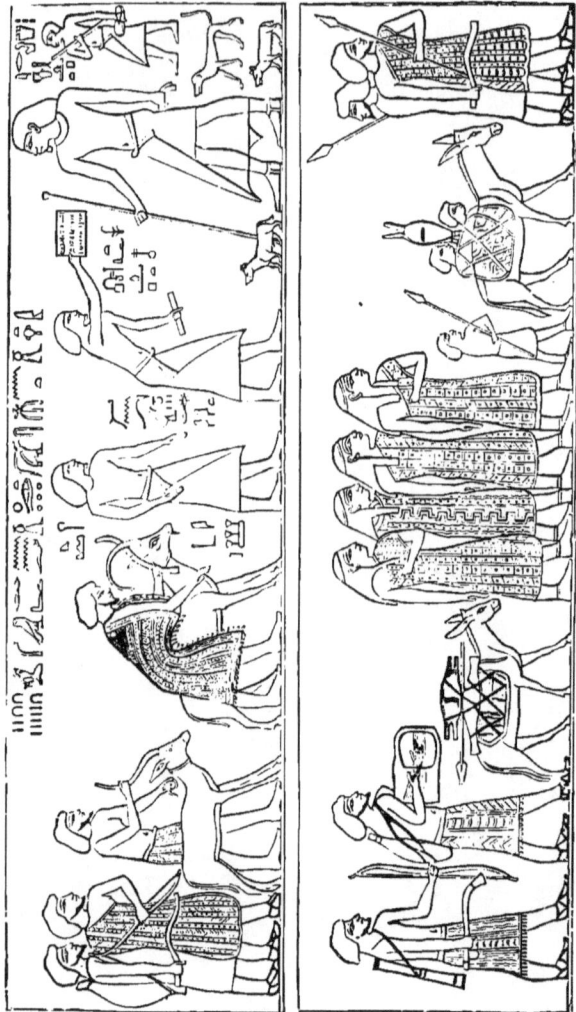

VISIT OF A FAMILY OF THE SEMITIC NATION CALLED AMU TO EGYPT.

(From the Tomb at Chnum-hetep.)

a famous wrestler. His attention was riveted by a series of wall-paintings, representing athletic sports, chiefly wrestling matches. I said to him, 'Are those pictures like the truth?' He replied enthusiastically, 'By Jove, there isn't a grip or a throw that I haven't used; and I defy the best wrestler in the north of England to do it better.'

In the tomb of Chnum-hetep the arrival of a party of Canaanitish shepherds in Egypt is depicted. They are being introduced to the monarch of the district by a scribe who holds a tablet, giving their number as

VALLEY OF THE NILE AT BENI HASSAN.

thirty-seven, and calling them *Amu;* by which name the Aramaic races were known to the Egyptians. A hieroglyphic inscription styles the leader of the party *Ilek-absh.* He is leading a Syrian goat as a present to the monarch, and in the panniers of the asses which follow are other presents, among them jars of stibium, at that time largely imported into Egypt from Palestine.[1] On its first discovery this fresco was supposed to represent the

---

[1] In the inscription it is said that they came from Bat Mestem, which probably means, 'the stibium mine.' A place of this name is mentioned in the Apocrypha as existing in the Plain of Jezreel.

coming down into Egypt of Jacob and his family. This opinion, now generally abandoned, was, however, strongly advocated at one of the early meetings of the Society of Biblical Archæology. It was shown that Jacob, his sons, their wives and children, give the exact number required, thirty-seven:

CHRISTIAN SYMBOLS AT BENI HASSAN.

the Biblical number of seventy-two being made up by concubines and their descendants; and it was maintained that *Hek-absh* is simply a transliteration into hieroglyphics of the Hebrew name, Jacob. A yet more startling view

SEBAK AND CHNUMIS.

was propounded at the same meeting. An eminent Egyptologist held it to be a record of the visit of Abraham. The date was asserted to be coincident with that of the Biblical narrative, and the name to be a translation of Abraham, meaning, 'the father of a multitude.' These identifications are doubtful; but the fresco is interesting, as a contemporary illustration of patriarchal history.

It has been mentioned that the rock-tombs of Egypt were used after the commencement of the Christian era as the abode of monks. Of this there are many curious traces at Beni Hassan. Among the ancient frescoes, we find Christian symbols, placed there by the anchorites, and closely resembling those in the Roman catacombs. In at least two cases we have the cross upon which doves are resting, symbolising the atoning

sacrifice of Christ, with the operations of the Spirit needful to give it effect
upon the hearts of men. One of these has a leaf of trefoil, typical of the
Trinity, and the Alpha and the Omega conjoined, so as to form a single
letter. The familiar monogram of Christ into which the cross is worked is

REMAINS OF THE TEMPLE AT ABYDOS.
(From Photograph by F. Frith.)

of frequent occurrence. Here, too, we find the mystic *Tau*, or *crux ansata* of
early Egyptian mythology, adopted as a Christian symbol. It is, at least, a
wonderful coincidence—perhaps more than a coincidence—that the cross
was the symbol of life among the Egyptians. The gods are constantly
represented as holding it in the right hand as shown in the engravings
on the opposite page. We cannot wonder that the early Christians should

have availed themselves of this significant fact to express their faith in
Him who by the cross 'abolished death, and hath brought life and
immortality to light.'

We have to ascend the Nile nearly three hundred and fifty miles above
Cairo, one hundred and sixty above Beni Hassan, before we reach any of the

THE GREAT HALL IN THE TEMPLE OF ABYDOS.

great temples of Ancient Egypt. Below this point they have all been
destroyed, and only their foundations can be traced. But from Girgeh up
to Abû-Simbel the number and magnificence of their remains give an impressive sense of the splendour of the kingdom of the Pharaohs. The first we
reach is that of Abydos, specially dedicated to Osiris, and which contended
with Philæ for the honour of being his place of burial. A donkey-ride of

PORTICO OF THE TEMPLE OF DENDERAH.

ten or twelve miles from Girgeh across a plain of extraordinary fertility, brings us to the edge of the desert. Here are the ruins of two temples, and the mounds which cover the vast cemetery around the tomb of the deified monarch. A superstitious feeling, like that which has prevailed in many lands and through successive ages, led the ancient Egyptians to seek sepulture in or near the sacred spot. The smaller of the two temples was of extraordinary richness and beauty. It was built of polished granite, lined with Oriental alabaster, still glowing with the colours which adorned it nearly four thousand years ago.[1]

The larger temple, erected by Seti, the father of Rameses II., is partly buried in the sand, which, whilst it conceals, has also preserved from injury so many remains of ancient magnificence. The colossal walls and columns which have been laid bare are decorated with sculptures and paintings. They record or depict the exploits of the king. We see him treading down his enemies at the head of his victorious armies, or worshipping the gods, or doing homage to his ancestors. In other parts of the building he is represented as eagerly engaged in the excitement of the chase, all the incidents of which are given; amongst others, a wild bull has been lassoed, whose struggles to get free are represented with wonderful spirit.

Between Girgeh and Denderah, our next halting-place, we pass the shrine of Sheikh Selim, one of the Moslem saints who in every age have thriven upon the superstitious credulity of the Egyptians. He is believed neither to eat, drink, nor sleep, but to spend his whole time in prayer and meditation. As we approached the spot, our crew began to collect money amongst themselves. Having got together a goodly heap of piastres, they tied them up in a handkerchief, and brought the boat as near the shore as they could with safety. A gang of ruffianly-looking Arabs, the attendants of the saint, now made their appearance, and with shouts and gesticulations demanded backsheesh in the name of their master. The parcel of coin being thrown to them, a violent scuffle took place for its possession, which continued till they had reached the hut of the saint. In reply to my expression of surprise at the large amount of money collected, I was told that on their last voyage the crew had neglected to make the usual contribution, and, as a consequence, every window on board had been broken by Sheikh Selim's curse, and the boat had run aground on a mud-bank in the river, where she lay for thirty-six hours before she could be got off. Our dragoman, an

BRICK WITH THE CARTOUCHE OF RAMESES II.

[1] It was from this temple that the famous tablet of Abydos was brought, which forms one of the most valuable treasures of the British Museum.

unbelieving Maltese, gave me a droll account of the piles of provisions brought by the peasantry to this fasting saint, adding, with a roguish twinkle of the eye, 'And yet I firmly believe that he never eats anything—except geese and turkeys.'

The great temple of Denderah is about sixty miles above Abydos. It was dedicated to Athor, the Egyptian Venus, and belongs to the later and degraded period of architecture, when the Pharaohs had been superseded by the Ptolemies and the Cæsars. A curious interest attaches to its date. In the early part of the present century, one of the zodiacs which ornament the roof, being examined by the French *savans*, was supposed to indicate an antiquity so great as to be incompatible with the Biblical narrative of the Creation and the Flood. Learned and elaborate arguments were constructed to prove that the Nile Valley must have been peopled by a highly-civilised race at a period long anterior to the existence of man upon the earth, as recorded in the Book of Genesis. But in their eager haste to disprove the authority of the Mosaic writings, the Egyptologists strangely overlooked the fact that the walls of the temple afford conclusive proof that, so far from going back to a mythical antiquity, it is scarcely older than the Christian era, having been commenced by Cleopatra and not completed till the reign of Nero.

THE RAMESSEUM, THEBES.

The vast size, the almost perfect preservation, and the sumptuous adornments of the temple make it very impressive. But it wants the severe and simple grandeur of the older edifices. It is overloaded with ornament, not in the best taste, and is a formal and florid imitation of the edifices of an earlier age. Sculptured upon the walls are portraits of Cleopatra, of colossal size. They are far from supporting her reputation for beauty. The face is expressive of sensuality and voluptuousness, and bears no trace of the ambition and intelligence with which she had been credited. Their resemblance to the original has sometimes been called in question, but, as Dean Stanley remarks, 'the fat full features are well brought out, and being like those at Hermonthis, give the impression that it must be a likeness.'

We are now approaching Thebes, the capital of Ancient Egypt, and the culminating point of its splendour and magnificence. Throughout a period nearly twice the length of our own history the wealth and power of successive Pharaohs had been devoted to its aggrandisement, and the labour of subdued and enslaved nations been employed in the erection of its temples and palaces. For fifteen hundred years each succeeding generation added something to its glories. Its Titanic edifices record the history and illustrate the greatness of the people throughout the whole period of their national existence.

The great plain of Thebes afforded a noble site for such a city. The Arabian and Libyan Mountains which enclose the Nile Valley here assume grander forms than in the northern parts of the chain, and they recede farther from the river, so as to inclose an amphitheatre of considerable extent, through the centre of which the river runs with a broad expanse of verdure on either bank. Within the area inclosed by these mighty bulwarks stood edifices, the ruins of which fill the spectator with awe-struck wonder. Avenues of statues and sphinxes, miles in length, ran along the plain, leading to propylons a hundred feet in height, through which kings and warriors, priests and courtiers, passed into the temples and palaces which lay beyond. Above all towered the colossal images of the Pharaohs, looking down upon the city, and far over the plain at their feet, like gigantic warders. As I wandered day after day with ever-growing amazement amongst these relics of ancient magnificence, I felt that if all the ruins in Europe - Classical, Celtic, and Mediæval—were brought together into one centre, they would fall far short both in extent and grandeur of those of this single Egyptian city.

Its original name was T-Ape, the head or capital, of which Thebes is a corruption. By the Hebrews it was known as No-Amon, the abode of Amon, the god to whom it was specially dedicated. References to its greatness and prophecies of its downfall are frequent in Scripture. Among the most striking of these is that of Nahum, when, taunting Nineveh, he says: 'Art thou better than No-Amon that was situated by the rivers, that had the waters round about it, whose rampart was the sea-like stream, and whose wall was the sea-like stream ? Ethiopia and Egypt were her strength, and it was infinite ; Put and Lubim were her helpers. Yet she was carried away, she went into captivity.' [1] The present desolation of the magnificent city affords an emphatic commentary on the denunciations of prophecy.

To depict and describe in detail the stupendous ruins which cover the great Theban plain would require many volumes like the present. We can only glance at some of the most important.

On the western bank, in what was called the Libyan suburb stands the great temple-palace known as the Ramesseum, or Memnonium. It was built by Rameses II., whose favourite title, Mi-Amon, the beloved of Amon, was probably corrupted by the Greeks into Memnon, and in this form

OSIRIDE COLUMNS OF RAMESSEUM, THEBES.

has passed into the languages of modern Europe. We can yet read upon its walls the achievements of the great king. We see him leading on his armies, slaughtering his enemies, receiving the spoils of captured cities, or peacefully administering his mighty empire, then co-extensive with the known world. Over all towered the colossal image of Pharaoh himself. No description, no measurement, gives any adequate idea of the bulk of this

---

[1] Nahum iii. 8-10. The prophet seems here to be speaking of the future and foreseen desolation of Thebes, as though it were already accomplished : but the date of Nahum's prophecy is very uncertain.

enormous statue, now prostrate in the dust. It was formed out of a block of syenite granite, estimated to weigh when entire nearly nine hundred tons.

PALACE OF RAMESES III., MEDINET-ABÛ.

It measures twenty-two feet from shoulder to shoulder; a toe is three feet long, the foot five feet across. It is now generally agreed that this was the king who 'knew not Joseph' and who so cruelly oppressed the Israelites. His mummy was discovered at Deir-el-Bahari, in 1881.[1]

Near the Ramesseum are the temples of Medinet-Abû, that is, as it should be understood, the city of Thebes. The largest of this group of buildings was erected by Rameses III., the last of the great warrior-kings of Egypt, about 1200 B.C. As in the case of his predecessors, we can trace his history on the walls of the temple. The glowing words of Lord Lindsay do not exaggerate the impressiveness of this marvellous edifice : 'I will only say that all I had anticipated of Egyptian magnificence fell short of the reality, and that it was here, surveying those Osiride pillars, that splendid corridor, with its massy circular columns ;

PALACE OF RAMESES III., MEDINET-ABÛ.

those walls lined, within and without, with historical sculpture of the deepest interest, the monarch's wars with the Eastern nations bordering on the Caspian and Bactriana—study for months, years rather !—it was here, I say, here, where almost every peculiarity of Egyptian architecture is assembled in

[1] See Section IV. of this volume.

THE COLOSSI OF THEBES.

perfection, that I first learnt to appreciate the spirit of that extraordinary people, and to feel that poetless as they were, they *had* a national genius, and had stamped it on the works of their hands, lasting as the *Iliad*. Willing slaves to the vilest superstition, bondsmen to form and circumstance, adepts in every mechanical art that can add luxury or comfort to human existence, yet triumphing abroad over the very Scythians, captives from every quarter of the globe figuring in those long oblational processions to the sacred shrines in which they delighted, after returning to their native Nile—that grave, austere, gloomy architecture, sublime in outline and heavily elaborate in ornament, what a transcript was it of their own character! And never were pages more graphic. The gathering, the march, the *mêlée*—the Pharaoh's prowess, standing erect, as he always does, in his car—no charioteer —the reins attached to his waist—the arrow drawn to his ear—his horses all fire, springing into the air like Pegasuses—and then the agony of the dying, transfixed by his darts, the relaxed limbs of the slain ; and, lastly, the triumphant return, the welcome home, and the offerings of thanksgiving to Amon, the fire, the discrimination with which these ideas are bodied forth must be seen to judge of it.'

Adjoining the temple are the ruins of a pyramidal tower, the internal arrangements and sculptures of which show that it was the palace of Rameses. It is remarkable as being almost the only instance yet discovered of an ancient dwelling. The Egyptians built their temples and tombs for eternity. Their own houses were constructed of perishable materials, to last only for the brief period of their continuance on earth. The rooms are small, but richly decorated. We see the king surrounded by the ladies of his court, who fan him, present him with flowers, and pay him court. In one place he is seen playing a game of chess, or draughts, with his attendants. The draught-men and the chequered board, though sculptured on the walls more than three thousand years ago, are similar to those used at the present day.

Seated in solemn and solitary majesty in the plain between the temples of Medinet-Abû and the river, are the two ' Colossi.' They alone remain of an avenue of eighteen similar statues which led up to the temple of Amenophis III. Though much broken and shattered, they present an aspect of wonderful grandeur. The following are the measurements as given by Murray : eighteen feet three inches across the shoulders : sixteen feet six inches from the top of the shoulder to the elbow ; ten feet six inches from the top of the head to the shoulder ; seventeen feet nine inches from the elbow to the finger's end ; nineteen feet eight inches from the knee to the plant of the foot. When entire, they must have risen to a height of sixty feet from the surrounding plain. They are thus somewhat smaller than the prostrate statue of Rameses, are of inferior workmanship, and carved out of a coarser material. One of them was partially overthrown either by Cambyses, the great Persian conqueror, or by an earthquake ; it has, however, been restored, though the traces of the injury are evident. They were seated upon their thrones when the Israelites were in Egypt, and they seem likely to remain there to the end of the world. One of them, known as the Vocal Memnon, was believed to emit a musical sound as the rays of the rising sun fell upon it, or in the presence of distinguished visitors. Various explanations were offered of this phenomenon, such as the trickling of sand amongst the cracks of the figure, or a slight movement of its parts caused by a change of temperature. The mystery was dispelled by Sir Gardner

COLUMNS OF TEMPLE AT LUXOR.

Wilkinson, who discovered in the lap of the figure a slab of stone, which, on being struck, gives out the exact sound described by Strabo and others.[1] For a trifling backsheesh, an Arab climbs up the statue, and, unseen by persons in the plain below, produces as often as is wished the note 'like the breaking of an harp string,' which was thrice repeated in honour of the Emperor Hadrian on his visit to Thebes.

Crossing the river to Luxor, which lies on the opposite bank, we find

[1] But see an article in the *Quarterly Review* for April 1875, maintaining the correctness of the first of these explanations.

an Arab village, built within and upon the temples of Amenophis III. and Rameses II. The effect is grotesque, and detracts sorely from their impressiveness. The silence and the sense of loneliness, which elsewhere give such a weird solemnity to the ruins, are here dispelled by the miserable hovels which cluster round the stately columns, and the swarms of beggars clamorously demanding backsheesh. There is, however, one part of the ruins

LUXOR.

remote from the village which is not infested by these annoyances, and here it is possible to admire the graceful, yet massive columns, and realise, in some measure, what Egyptian architecture was in its most perfect period of development.

The temple-palaces of Luxor and Karnak were united by a magnificent avenue of sphinxes, which led for nearly two miles across the plain. The roadway between them was sixty-three feet in width, and as the sphinxes were only twelve feet apart, the number of these majestic figures was almost incredible. For fifteen hundred feet from Luxor, they were of the usual form, with female heads; thence to Karnak they were crio, or ram-headed sphinxes, as being sacred to Amon. A similar avenue led from the main front to a quay and flight of steps on the bank of the river, and eight or ten other approaches, not inferior in grandeur to these two, have been traced.

As we approach Karnak, the most striking objects are two of the enormous propylons so characteristic of Egyptian architecture. They are truncated pyramids, pierced with a gateway. The sides slope inward from a rectangular base, and are often surmounted by a heavy cornice, on which is sculptured the symbol known to the Greeks as the *Agathodæmon* a winged sun, or scarabæus, reminding us of the words of Scripture, 'He shall cover thee with His feathers, and under

PROPYLON AT KARNAK.

His wings shalt thou trust.'¹ It was the number of these propylons which gained for Thebes the Homeric epithet of 'the hundred-gated city.'

We now enter the most stupendous pile of remains— we can hardly call them ruins in the world. Every writer who has attempted to describe

¹ Psalm xci. 4.

them, avows his inability to convey any adequate idea of their extent and grandeur. The long, converging avenues of sphinxes, the sculptured corridors, the columned aisles, the gates, and obelisks, and colossal statues, all silent in their desolation, fill the beholder with awe. There is no exaggeration in Champollion's words : 'The imagination, which in Europe rises far above our porticoes, sinks abashed at the foot of the one hundred and forty columns of the hypostyle hall at Karnak.' The area of this hall is fifty-seven thousand six hundred and twenty-nine feet. The central columns are thirty-four feet in circumference and sixty-two feet in height, without reckoning the plinth and abacus. They are covered with paintings and sculptures, the colours of which are wonderfully fresh and vivid.

GREAT HALL AT KARNAK.

If, as seems probable, the great design of Egyptian architecture was to impress man with a feeling of his own littleness, to inspire a sense of overwhelming awe in the presence of the deity, and, at the same time, to show that the monarch was a being of superhuman greatness, these edifices were well adapted to accomplish their purpose. This has been well stated by Mr. Zincke in his suggestive work on Egypt. The Egyptian beholder and worshipper was not to be attracted and

charmed, but overwhelmed. His own nothingness, and the terribleness of
the power and will of God, was what he was to feel. But if the awfulness
of the deity was thus inculcated, the divine power of the Pharaoh was not
less striking-
ly set forth.
He is seen
seated a-
mongst the
gods, nou-
rished from
their breast,
folded in
their arms,
admitted to
familiar in-
tercourse
with them.
He is repre-
sented on the
walls of the
temples as of
colossal sta-
ture, whilst
the noblest
of his sub-
jects are but
pigmies in
his presence.
With one
hand he
crushes hosts
of enemies,
with the
other he
grasps that
of his patron
deity. The
Pharaoh was
the earthly

HYPOSTYLE HALL, KARNAK.

manifestation and *avatar* of the unseen and mysterious power which oppressed
the souls of men with terror. 'I am Pharaoh;' 'by the life of Pharaoh;'
'say unto Pharaoh, Whom art thou like in thy greatness?'[1] These familiar

[1] Genesis xli. 44; xlii. 15, 16; Ezekiel xxxi. 2. Quoted by Dean Stanley, in *Sinai and Palestine.*

phrases of Scripture gain a new emphasis of meaning as we remember them amongst these temple-palaces. It is with a feeling of relief that we turn away from these dread-inspiring deities to think of Him who 'dwelleth not in temples made with hands;' who calls Himself our Father, and who invites from us not the servile worship of terror, but a filial 'love which casteth out fear:' whose earthly manifestation and incarnation has been made, not in the person of a deified conqueror, but in one who was 'a Man of sorrows and acquainted with grief;' who 'is touched with a feeling of our infirmities;' who 'bare our sins in His own body on the tree.' and who is now exalted to the right hand of the Majesty on high, 'a Prince and a Saviour, to give repentance and the remission of sins.'

COLUMNS AND PART OF OBELISK OF THOTHMES III., KARNAK.

Amongst the temples of Karnak a special interest attaches to one comparatively late in date. but which is the earliest yet discovered which directly and certainly touches the history of other nations. Sheshank—the Shishak of Scripture—was one of the last of the Pharaohs who, for the space of more than a thousand years, had been busy building up the glories of Karnak. He erected a kind of chapel flanking the great portico toward the south, and, after the manner of his race, cut into its walls a record of his achievements. We see the colossal figure leading in bonds the pigmy monarchs whom he had conquered. On a cartouche is written, in hieroglyphics, the name of each. The sculptures, discovered and deciphered by Champollion, record that Shishak is dragging before the Theban trinity the types of more than thirty nations which he had subdued. From the variety of their features, they are evidently intended to be typical of the people represented. Amongst them is one with a distinctly Jewish cast of face. Turning to the Bible, we find that, ' In the fifth year of king Rehoboam, Shishak king of Egypt came up against Jerusalem, because they had transgressed against the Lord, with twelve hundred chariots, and threescore thousand horsemen, and people without number, and he took the fenced cities which pertained to Judah, and came to Jerusalem, and he took away the treasures of the house of the Lord, and the treasures of the king's house ; he took all.'¹ This monument may thus be a contemporary record of the event narrated in Scripture.

It has been already mentioned that the Egyptians built their houses of perishable materials, but that their temples and tombs were constructed on the grandest scale, and of the most enduring character. How true this is of the Theban temples we have seen. We now turn to the tombs, which are scarcely less wonderful in their extent and magnificence. They were constructed in the *háger*, that

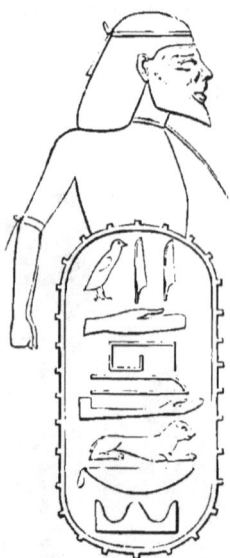

A CAPTIVE JEW OF SHISHAK'S TIME.

FRANÇOIS CHAMPOLLION.

¹ 1 Kings xiv. 25 ; 2 Chron. xii. 3 9.

is, 'a rock,' and refers to the rocky precipices which rise from the fertile banks of the river. Crossing the western plain, here about three miles in width, and leaving behind us the seated Colossi, and the temples of Kûrnah, Medinet-Abû, and the Ramesseum, we enter a savage gorge. The walls of rock on either side of the ravine, utterly denuded of soil, glow in the pitiless sunshine, like the mouth of a furnace. Overhead rises a pyramidal mass of rock, which forms a striking feature in the landscape, and commands from its summit a striking view of the Nile Valley and Desert. No tree, or blade of grass, or drop of water, or living thing is visible as the travellers pass

SCULPTURED WALL, KARNAK.

along in the blinding glare. This gorge leads us to the *Bibán el Moluk*, or tombs of the kings. The rocks are honeycombed with sepulchres, which run far into the mountain sides. Here the Theban Pharaohs 'lie in glory, every one in his own house.'[1] Near them are queens, priests, and nobles, interred with a splendour not inferior to that of the Pharaohs. Some of these sepulchral halls are of vast extent. One of them, that of the Assaseef, is eight hundred and sixty-two feet in length, without reckoning the lateral chambers; the total area of excavation is twenty-three thousand eight

[1] Isaiah xiv. 18.

hundred and nine feet, occupying an acre and a quarter of ground, 'an immoderate space for the sepulchre of one individual, even allowing that the members of his family shared a portion of its extent.'[1]

The sides of these tombs are covered with frescoes and sculptures,

SHISHAK AND HIS CAPTIVES ON SCULPTURED WALL AT KARNAK.

sometimes giving the portrait of the inmate and illustrating his career. More frequently, they are fancy sketches, or what we should call *genre* paintings. The life of the Egyptian people is here portrayed with extraordinary accuracy and detail. 'We saw here, as in a picture story-book, how the man had

[1] For details of the recent wonderful discoveries in this region, see Section IV. of this volume.

cultivated his gardens and fields, had garnered his harvests, had sent merchandise on the river in boats sailing with the wind— how he had gone to battle and taken the command of armies— the gathering in of his vintage, the games and shoutings of the wine-pressers, his sports in fishing and fowling. Then we saw him—a picture of easy joy—in the midst of the family circle. We saw him at the feast: guests were at his dwelling; he welcomed them to the merry banquet; slaves crowned them with garlands of flowers; the wine-cup passed round. Then there were harpers and musicians and players on the double pipes. Girls in long wavy hair and light clinging garments were dancing. But to all things there comes an end. We saw here, also, the day (how far back in the depths of time!) when those pleasant

TOMBS OF THE KINGS AT THEBES.

feasts were all over—the lilies dead, the music hushed. the last of this man's harvest stored, the last trip enjoyed by boat or chariot. The fish need no more fear him in the pools, nor the fowl among the reeds. Here he was lying under the hands of the embalmers. And next we saw him in mummy form on the bier, in the consecrated boat which was to carry him over the dark river and land him at the gates of the heavenly abode, where the genii of the dead and Osiris were awaiting him to try his deeds, and pronounce his sentence for eternal good or ill.'[1]

[1] *Leisure Hour,* May 1867.

Standing among the affecting memorials of lives, the earthly course of which was terminated thousands of years ago, we ask ourselves what knowledge or hope had they of the life to come ?   They distinctly recognised the great

FRESCOES IN TOMBS OF THE KINGS AT THEBES.

facts of a judgment after death, the immortality of the soul, and the resurrection of the body.   The practice of embalming the dead was indeed but an expression of this belief, which was wrought into their whole habit of thought and mode of life.   We learn this not merely from the inscriptions in

HARPER IN TOMB AT THEBES.

the tombs, temples, and on the sarcophagi, but from rolls of papyrus placed with the mummy in the coffin, which trace the course of the disembodied spirit to the regions of reward or punishment.   In one chapter of these Books of the Dead, as they are called, we see the spirit hovering over the corpse in the form of a hawk, with human head and hands, and grasping the symbol of life and stability.   The body is borne across the river, accompanied by priests and mourners to the grave.   The spirit passes away to *Amenti.*   Here it encounters innumerable perils from the monsters which lie in wait to avenge upon it any crimes of which it has been guilty during life.   The prayers and protestations of innocence which are to prove its safeguard are dictated.   Then it enters the judgment hall of Osiris.   Here are seen the forty-two judges of the dead.   Some are human, others have the heads of the crocodile, hawk, lion, ape, etc.   Before them kneels the dead man repeating the negative confession from which we extract the following : ' I have defrauded no man : I have not prevaricated at the seat of justice : I have not made slaves of the Egyptians : I have not defiled my conscience for the sake of my superior : I have not used violence : I have not famished my household : I have not made to weep : I have not committed forgery : I have not falsified weights or measures : I have not pierced the banks of the Nile, nor separated for myself an arm of the Nile in its increase : I have not been gluttonous : I have not been drunken :' etc.   In the lower tier is the judgment hall of Osiris. We see on the right three figures.   The one in the centre, clothed in the usual

IN THE TOMBS AT THEBES.

Egyptian dress, is the dead man.   He is received by two females, each with an ostrich feather in her headdress, symbolising Law.   One introduces him to the other, who holds a sceptre and a *crux ansata*—the symbols of authority and life.   In the centre is the balance of judgment.   The heart is placed in one scale, the symbols of truth and justice in the other.   One of the ministers of Thoth, the scribe of the gods cynocephalus, in the form of an ape, whose name is Hap (sentence, judgment), sits on the stand which supports the balance.   Horus, the hawk-headed, the beloved son of Osiris and Anubis, watch the scale in which the heart is placed, and at

the same time closely observes the index of the balance. The opposite scale
is trimmed by the dog-headed Anubis, who declares the result of the scrutiny
to the ibis-headed Thoth, the divine wisdom, who stands with his writing-
tablet and pen in front of Osiris, the supreme judge of this fearful assize,
and records the sentence in his presence. Osiris himself is seated in a shrine
on the extreme left, and wears a diadem adorned with two ostrich feathers,
and with the disk of the sun and the horns of a goat. He holds a whip
and a crook-headed sceptre, symbolising justice and law. Immediately
before the throne, and within the shrine, is a stand, upon which is hung

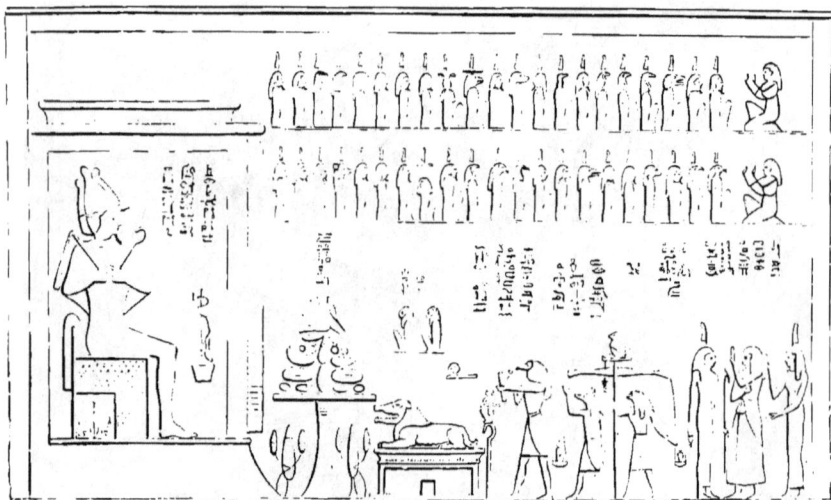

THE JUDGMENT HALL OF OSIRIS.

the skin of a panther: the meaning of this is unknown. An altar laden
with offerings, and surmounted by the lotus-flower, stands in front of the
shrine. It probably represents the acts of piety performed on behalf of
the deceased by his surviving relatives. On the pedestal before the throne
a monster crouches, with the paws of a lion and the head of a crocodile
and the body of a horse; his name, 'the Devourer of Amenti,' as well as
his appearance, point him out as another of the ministers of vengeance
executing the judgments of the divinity before whom he crouches.

The sentence pronounced was full of joy to the good, and of woe to
the wicked. They who, by the faithful discharge of their duties a schildren,
as parents, as masters or servants, as kings or subjects, had been enabled

to pass the ordeal, were admitted to the habitations of blessedness, where they rested from their labours. Here they reap the corn and gather the fruits of paradise under the eye and smile of the lord of joy, that is, the sun, who exhorts them thus : ' Take your sickles, reap your grain, carry it into your dwellings, and be glad therewith, and present it a pure offering to the god.' There also they bathe in the pure river of life that flows past their habita- tions. Over them is inscribed : ' They have found favour in the eyes of the great god, they inhabit the mansions of glory, where they enjoy the life of heaven ; the bodies which they have abandoned shall repose in their tombs while they rejoice in the presence of the supreme god.'

The system of eschatology, thus sketched in the briefest possible outline, suggests many questions of profound interest, to which, however, no adequate reply can at present be given. Whence was it derived ? Is it a distorted tradition of some primeval revelation made to man ; or is it but a part of that universal illumination of the Holy Spirit, which ' enlightening every man that cometh into the world,' never leaves God without a witness even in the heart of the heathen, ' so that they are without excuse ? ' It is easy for us to discover a symbolism in the forms in which these beliefs were embodied. For instance, we may see in the monsters which avenged the different vices and crimes upon offenders, the types of those vices and crimes them- selves, thus suggesting the truth that those sins brought with them their own

SOUL VISITING ITS BODY, AND HOLDING THE EMBLEMS OF LIFE AND BREATH IN ITS CLAWS.

punishment. How far did the Egyptians understand these deeper and more spiritual teachings ? This doctrine of a future state of rewards and punish- ments was fully developed at the time when Moses was ' learned in all the wisdom of the Egyptians.' It must have been known to him. How comes it, then, that truths which hold so prominent a place in the later Scriptures, should be almost, or altogether, passed over in his writings ? This is one of those unexplained silences of Scripture for the explanation of which we must wait in faith and patience. We cannot but note yet further the in- sufficiency of the knowledge thus possessed to bring peace and pardon to the guilty. The ritual of the dead tells us that the innocent man shall be ' justified ' in the judgment hall of Osiris. ' Where, then, shall the sinner and the ungodly appear ? ' It was reserved for Him who ' brought life and immortality to light,' and who ' gave Himself a ransom for us,' to reveal the way of the sinner's acceptance with God through faith in Him ' that justifieth the ungodly.'

Before leaving the tombs at Thebes, it is necessary to refer to one which is supposed to contain a record of the captivity of the Israelites in Egypt. A gang of slaves are engaged in brickmaking, under the eye of a taskmaster, who is seated, staff in hand, superintending their labours. That they belong to a Semitic race is evident. But that the Jews were ever settled so high up the Nile Valley is very doubtful. Pithom and Raamses, the treasure cities which they are said to have built, were on the north-eastern frontier in the land of Goshen,[1] and their name does not occur amongst those of the nations recorded in this tomb. The painting is, however, interesting as illustrating the condition of a people compelled 'to serve with rigour in mortar and in brick, and in all manner of service in the field.'[2]

ERMENT, OR HERMONTHIS, NEAR THEBES.

Leaving Thebes reluctantly, and feeling that months might be spent in exploring its remains, we pursue our course up the Nile, and reach Esneh. Here is a temple, the portico of which has been excavated only in the present century. The sand in which it was so long buried has preserved

[1] Exodus i. 11.   [2] Exodus i. 13, 14.

its sculptures and paintings in marvellous perfection. The colours are as fresh and bright as when laid on at the commencement of the Christian era. It belongs to the later period of Egyptian art, when it had come decidedly under Greek influence. The present edifice probably occupies the site of an older one, built by Thothmes III. The palm leaf here replaces the lotus in the capitals of the columns, which are of great beauty. No two are alike. Their variety and grace afford a fine study for the decorative artist. We may observe here the change which had passed over the Egyptian feeling towards the gods and Pharaohs, since the time when they were regarded with awe and terror. Greek thought and feeling had human-

PORTICO AND TEMPLE AT ESNEH.

ised the deities, and brought them down from their mysterious seclusion into friendly intercourse with man. In one panel we see them assisting the monarchs in the sports of the field. They are holding the cords of a clap-net in four divisions. The upper tier encloses flying birds; the second, birds perched among the trees; the third, water-fowl; the fourth, fishes. In another section, the gods, with their characteristic head-dresses and symbols of authority, are driving bulls, goats, and flocks of geese. Whilst the form of Egyptian worship remained, the sense of reverence and awe, which formed its spirit and essence, had departed.

About thirty miles above Esneh is the most perfectly preserved temple

K

in Egypt—that of Edfou. Until excavated by M. Mariette, in 1864, only the
propylons were visible; the rest was hidden beneath an Arab village which
had been built upon its walls and sanctuary. It belongs to the period of the
Ptolemies, and, like the temple at Esneh, exhibits the gods engaged in field-
sports. One corridor is mainly devoted to harpooning the hippopotamus,
and, with the irresistible tendency of the Egyptians to caricature, many of
the incidents are very droll. In several cases the clumsy harpooner has
struck his weapon into one of the attendants, instead of the animal at

THE TEMPLE AT EDFOU.

which it was aimed. Doubtless there was a mythological meaning in the
sculptures—the hippopotamus being a symbol of Typhon, the Evil principle.
But the realism and the fun of the scene are strangely out of keeping with
the conventional and reverential tone of earlier art.

A few hours after leaving Edfou we reach Silsilis, which is interesting
as being the quarry from which the stone was cut for the temples and
palaces of Thebes. The excavations are of immense extent on both sides
of the river, which is here very narrow. They have been vividly described
by Eliot Warburton, who says : ' Hollowed out of the rocks are squares as

large as that of St. James's, streets as large as Pall Mall, and lanes and alleys without number; in short, you have all the negative features of a town, if I may so speak, i.e., if a town be considered as a *cameo*, these quarries are a vast *intaglio*.' The tool-marks of the masons, made three thousand years ago, are distinctly visible, and it is easy to see the methods

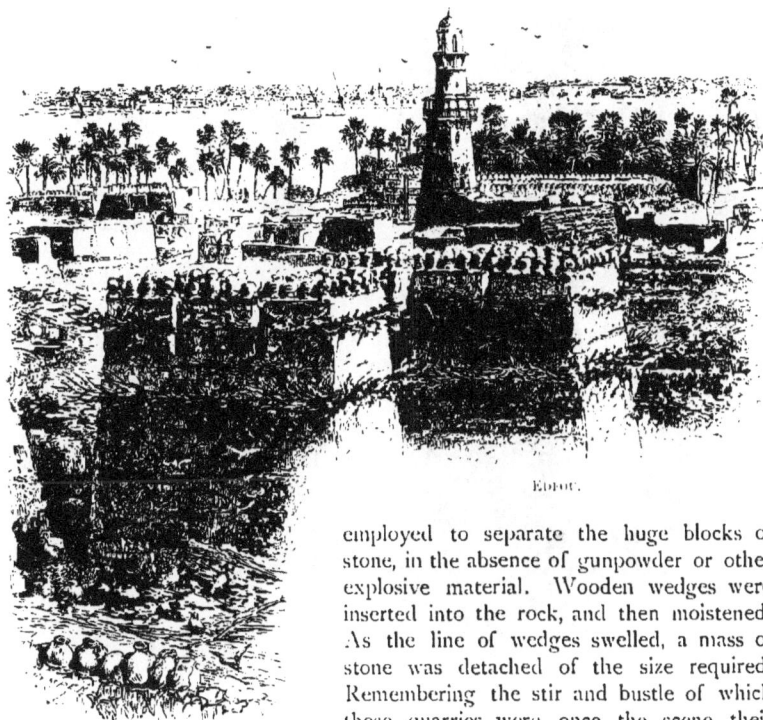

EDFOU.

employed to separate the huge blocks of stone, in the absence of gunpowder or other explosive material. Wooden wedges were inserted into the rock, and then moistened. As the line of wedges swelled, a mass of stone was detached of the size required. Remembering the stir and bustle of which these quarries were once the scene, their present solitude and silence are most impressive. Facing the river are a number of small grottoes or chapels, apparently for the use of the quarrymen, and these, with the buttresses of stone carved into the form of columns, have a very picturesque appearance, giving the impression of a vast city hewn out of the living rock.

Fifteen miles above Silsilis, we reach the temple of Kom Ombo.

K 2

Standing as it does on the summit of a hill overlooking the Nile Valley, it forms a very striking object from the river. Though small in size as compared with the mighty masses of Karnak and Luxor, it is one of the most beautiful edifices in Egypt. The sand-drift from the desert has buried the lower part of the columns, and threatens to submerge the whole. On the riverside the banks are being rapidly undermined by the force of the current. One smaller temple lower down the slope has already been swept away, and apparently in a few years this too will disappear.

We now approach the first cataract of the Nile. The scenery begins to assume a more distinctively Nubian

GROTTOES OF SILSILIS.

character. Soon the ruined towers over Assouan come into view, and the second stage of our journey is completed.

ASSOUAN TO ABU-SIMBEL.

A KAFIR WOMAN

LANDING-PLACE AT ASSOUAN.

SECTION III.

ASSOUAN TO ABU-SIMBEL.

THE approach to Assouan is very picturesque, and affords a pleasing contrast to the scenery of the Lower and Middle Nile. Instead of flat monotonous banks of sand and mud, we have masses of rock, broken up into grotesque and fantastic forms. Groves of palm, mimosa, and castor-oil plant come down to the water's edge. The limestone and sandstone ranges which hem in the Nile Valley from Cairo to Silsilis, give place to granite, porphyry, and basalt. The islands in the stream are no longer shifting accretions of mud, alternately formed and dissolved by the force of the current, but rocks and boulders of granite, which rise high above the river and resist its utmost force. The ruined convents and towers which crown the hills might almost cheat us into the belief that we were afloat on the Rhine or the Moselle, but for the tropical character of the scenery.

This altered aspect of the scenery is in accordance with the political geography of the district. We have reached the southern boundary of

Egypt, and are about to enter Nubia. The kingdom of the Pharaohs lies behind us, and we are on the borderland from which they marched for the conquest of Ethiopia. To this fact Ezekiel refers when, denouncing the Divine vengeance against Egypt, he says : ' Behold, therefore, I am against thee, and against thy rivers, and I will make the land of Egypt utterly waste and desolate, from Migdol to Syene, even the border of Ethiopia.' [1]

Assouan is a great centre for traffic with the interior. Caravans arrive from the desert, the camels are unloaded, and in a few days start again with consignments of manufactured articles—prints, beads, guns, powder—for barter with the native tribes. Dhows from Nubia and the Soudan, too heavily laden to descend the cataract, discharge their cargoes near Philæ, to be borne overland to this point for transhipment to Cairo or Alexandria.

ISLAND OF ELEPHANTINE.

A broad open space outside the town, on the bank of the river, serves at once as warehouse and exchange. Arabs, Turks, Negroes, Nubians, Abyssinians meet here on a footing of perfect equality. Trade levels all distinctions. Many of them are camped in native fashion. Bales of goods are arranged in a circle, so as to form a rampart against attack. In the centre a fire is kindled for cooking, around which the women and children lounge, whilst the men are chaffering in the bazaars, or gossiping on the beach. All the products of Central Africa may be bought here—elephants' tusks, odoriferous gums, ostrich feathers, ebony, clubs, poisoned arrows, shields of rhinoceros hide, strange birds, monkeys, and sometimes lions. I was asked fifteen pounds for a lion cub, about the size of a Newfoundland dog.

[1] Ezekiel xxix. 10, *margin.* Migdol was the frontier town on the north-east, as Syene, or Assouan, was on the south.

Failing to find a purchaser, the owner gradually came down to four pounds; but it remained unsold. It was a good-tempered little brute, playing about like a huge over-grown kitten, but an angry growl and ominous showing of the teeth gave warning of trouble at no distant period.

Opposite Assouan is the Island of Elephantine, or, as it is called by the natives, Gezeeret ez Zaher, the Island of Flowers. It formed an outpost for the successive lords of Egypt—Pharaohs, Ptolemies, Cæsars, and Saracen Caliphs—all of whom have left traces of their military occupation. The temples and the Nilometer, which, up to 1822, stood on the island, have almost disappeared, having been used as a quarry by the Governor of Assouan to build himself a palace. Only a few fragments now remain to excite our indignation against the vandalism of the destroyer.

In continuing our journey from Assouan and Elephantine to Philæ, we may either ride across the desert or ascend the cataract. If we adopt the former route, we shall probably have our first experience of camel-riding, and it will be far from agreeable. The animal has a peculiar gait, lifting both feet on the same side together, instead of the near fore-leg and off hind-leg, like the horse. This gives a peculiar corkscrew motion to the spine of the rider, which becomes absolutely painful after a short time. Immediately on leaving the town we pass the old Saracenic cemetery. Like all those of Modern Egypt, it is in a state of extreme neglect and dilapidation. The dead are covered with a thin sprinkling of earth, scarcely sufficient to protect them from the ravages of hyenas and jackals. The modern burial-places thus offer a striking contrast to the imperishable monuments in which the embalmed bodies were deposited by the ancient Egyptians. We soon reach the quarries from which the huge blocks of syenite granite were hewn for the temples of Lower Egypt. As at Silsilis, the quarry marks of the workmen are yet distinctly visible, and the vast extent of the excavations gives an impressive sense of the scale upon which the old builders worked. An obelisk yet remains in the quarry; it is about a hundred feet in height, by eleven feet two inches in breadth. When, and by whom it was cut out from the rock, and why it was left here instead of being removed to its destined site, cannot now be known. A similar mass of stone, hewn, squared, and prepared for removal, is found in the quarries near Baalbec.

The road now enters a savage defile, even more stern and desolate than that leading to the Tombs of the Kings at Thebes. Bare granite rocks rise on either hand. The bed of the *wady* is strewn with granite boulders lying in wild confusion, many of them inscribed with hieroglyphics and sculptures. Traces of ruined fortifications are visible, intended either to protect traders from the attack of marauding Bedouin, or to close the pass against invading hordes from the south. Emerging from the defile of rock and sand, and crossing a strip of desert, we reach the banks of the river above the cataract. A clump of magnificent sycamores affords grateful shade after a hot and weary ride, and Philæ, with its exquisite loveliness, more than fulfils our highly-raised expectations.

Before describing the other route to Philæ, it is necessary to explain that by the Cataracts of the Nile, all that is meant is a series of rapids which rush down from just below the Island of Biggeh, to just above Elephantine. There is no actual cascade or cataract, in our sense of the word, but the river boils and rages along the narrow channel, and whirls in dangerous eddies around the rocks and islets which obstruct its course. From the language of Cicero and Seneca it seems probable that two thousand years ago the fall was greater than it is now. After making allowance for the exaggerations into which classical writers fell when describing strange and unfamiliar scenes, it is difficult to suppose that they only saw what we now see.

If the river be not too low, and the wind be fair, there is abundant excitement, but no real danger, in the ascent of the cataracts. The daha-bieh sails smoothly on between the rocky islets above Elephantine till the first rapid is reached. This is commonly passed without any difficulty, if there be a good steady breeze. It is at the second rapid that the struggle begins. The rowers strain at their oars till they bend almost to breaking. Long poles are thrust out against every rock in the channel to gain a purchase. The boatmen leap into the seething cauldron to carry a rope to some pro-jecting headland, whence they may haul the vessel against the current. The *reïs* shouts and gesticulates to the crew like a madman. Sometimes the boat is caught in an eddy, whirled round, and seems to be on the point of de-struction, but a shifting of the broad lateen sail, a turn of the helm, or the coiling of a rope round a mass of rock makes all right again. It is a scene of indescribable confusion. Everybody is bawling at the top of his voice. The orders of the *reïs* are drowned in the hurly-burly. At length, by dint of poling and warping, the top of the rapid is reached, and the vessel floats in smooth water once again. The current still runs strong, and vigorous rowing is needed for some distance, till we find ourselves off the village of Mahatta, and close upon the temple-crowned island which is our destination.

Scarcely less exciting than the ascent of the rapids by a dahabiyyeh, is the sight of the Nubians descending them. The people of the district ordinarily cross the river astride on a log of wood. Even little children paddle themselves to and fro with marvellous skill. Stripping off their clothing, if they have any, and making it up into a bundle to carry on their heads, they move about in the water as though it were their native element. Afloat in the river on these rude aboriginal rafts, a score of men will let themselves be drawn down by the current into the maddest rush and whirl of the rapid, and having reached its foot, swim ashore and beg for backsheesh, which is seldom refused.

The Island of Philæ, which lies just above the first cataract, was sacred to Osiris, the most prominent figure in the Egyptian Pantheon. The legends concerning him formed the centre of the Egyptian mythological system.

The island is covered with temples, but none of them are older than the era of the Ptolemies. The original edifices were destroyed by Persian iconoclasts, and very few traces of them can be discovered. It is difficult to make out the general plan of the buildings. What Sir Gardner Wilkinson called the 'symmetrophobia' of the Egyptians is here most strikingly illustrated. Where

AMEN, ISIS, AND CHONSU.

a modern architect would secure a magnificent vista by avenues leading in straight lines to a central and commanding point, they broke up the ground-plan into detached and unsymmetrical portions. No part of the edifice corresponded in design to any other part. Propylons, gateways, side-chapels, seem to have been placed just where the whim of the builder dictated, with little or no regard to the production of an harmonious and well-balanced whole. This is specially true of the edifices on Philæ.

HEAD OF BES.

The most conspicuous building on the island is a hypæthral hall, near the landing-place, vulgarly known as Pharaoh's bed. It is detached from the main temple, and its builder and purpose are alike unknown. It can hardly have been a temple, and may possibly have been erected merely as an architectural feature. The most probable view is that it was a comparatively modern erection over the assumed grave of Osiris. Its situation is very striking, and it harmonises well with the surrounding scenery; but I should hardly go the length of Mr. Fairholt, who pronounces it 'the most exquisite in its effect of any in Egypt.'

ISIS COLUMNS WITH EASTERN COLONNADE AND PYLON.

The great temple of Isis was approached by a quay and a flight of steps leading up from the river at the southern end of the island. The visitor then passed between a pair of obelisks, of which only one is now standing, and along an avenue of Isis-headed columns to the great propylon. A peristyle court and a small temple, sacred to Horus, are then entered; another smaller propylon succeeds, and we reach the grand portico of the temple of Isis, its columns glowing with colour, their capitals delicately and exquisitely designed from lotus, acacia, and palm leaves. This general plan, however, fails to give any idea of the bewildering mazes of corridors, halls, and shrines, which succeed one another. Perhaps the most interesting portion of the building is a small chapel constructed upon the roof of one of the terraces. The sculptures in this chamber represent the history of Osiris. We see the mangled remains of the slain monarch brought together, women are weeping round his bier, whilst the symbol of the soul hovers over the corpse. Gradually the signs of returning life are indicated. Winged figures, like the cherubim of Scripture, stand around, overshadowing and guarding the body with their wings. The mystic legend unfolds itself step by step, till Osiris is seen robed, crowned, seated upon his throne, bearing in his hands, which are crossed upon his breast, the insignia of empire, and

INTERIOR OF GREAT COURT.

he is installed as the mighty and beneficent ruler of the invisible world.

On the downfall of the Egyptian mythology, Philæ became an important Christian colony. The monks who settled here, like those at Beni Hassan, defaced the symbols of the old faith and substituted for them those of Christianity. Some of these are very curious. We have not only the cross of the ordinary form with the familiar addition of the palm branch of victory, or inclosed within a circle of amaranth, symbolising eternity, but we find strange combinations of unusual forms with fanciful additions, of which it is often difficult to discover the meaning. Thus the Jerusalem cross, as it is now called, appears with a semicircle on each of its arms, or with globes at each extremity and grouped round the centre. What looks at first like a mere arabesque or geometrical pattern resolves itself into a series of crosses, with that of St. Andrew in the centre, and triangles at each corner, as types of the Trinity. At this distance of time it is impossible to say how far these rude inscriptions were expressive

PORTICO OF TEMPLE AT PHILÆ.

of a true spiritual faith in the Divine verities thus symbolised. But from what we know of the character of the Egyptian monks, there is but too much reason to fear that they only represent a gross superstition scarcely more respectable than the heathenism they replaced. One great cause of the

CHRISTIAN SYMBOLS AT PHILÆ.

rapid spread of Mohammedanism in the seventh century was the idolatry and degraded superstition into which the Church had then fallen. And at the present day one main hindrance to the progress of Christianity amongst the Moslems is their deep-rooted belief that it is essentially idolatrous—a belief created and fostered by the creed and ritual of the Greek, Latin, and Coptic churches. Slowly this erroneous idea is being dispelled by the teaching of Protestant evangelists. But everywhere throughout the Mohammedan world, I have found that the worship of the crucifix, of Mary, and of the saints, has raised an almost insuperable prejudice against Christianity. Strange that a faith which teaches that 'God

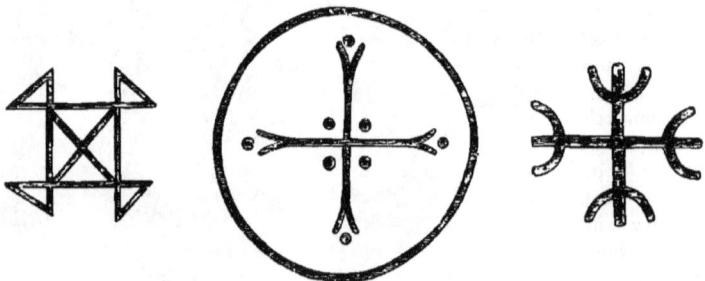

CHRISTIAN SYMBOLS AT PHILÆ.

is a Spirit: and they that worship Him must worship him in spirit and in truth,' should, by the misrepresentations of its avowed adherents, have been exposed to such a charge.

The general aspect of Nubian scenery is similar to that of Egypt, but with some marked differences. The Nile flows on through a valley with mountain ranges on either hand. Its banks, fertilised by the river, are of a

THE DOUM PALM IN NUBIA.

rich emerald green. Beyond this narrow strip of verdure all is bare rock and barren sand. But the mountain-sides are more precipitous, and come down nearer to the water's edge, thus diminishing the area to which the annual inundation rises, and, as a consequence, the cultivable soil is proportionately less. Artificial irrigation becomes more than ever needful, and sakiehs and shadoofs are seen all along the river banks. The population is scanty. The soil indeed is wonderfully productive, but there is so little of it, that large numbers are com-
pelled to emigrate to Cairo or Alexandria, and find employment as water-carriers, donkey-drivers, or labourers. The cottages are often mere walls of baked mud, covered with thatch, with only a

MUD HUTS.

single chamber in each. Some of the sheikhs' houses, however, are very picturesque, and are built in the curious fashion which we have seen in Upper Egypt. The upper parts are ornamented with bands of plaster cornices, and rows of earthen pots are let into the walls, to serve as pigeon-houses.

The landscape has been gradually becoming more tropical in character, so that we actually enter the tropics a little way above Philæ without being conscious of any marked change. Doum palms, which we first saw just below Thebes, are striking features in the landscape. Some of them attain great size, and afford an agreeable contrast to the bare columnar stems of the date palm. Fields of maize, millet, cotton, and sugar-cane line the banks, and produce three harvests in the year, with little toil to the cultivator, beyond that re-

SHEIKH'S HOUSE.

quired for raising water from the river for purposes of irrigation. Most of the work in the fields is done by women and children. The men have either gone down into Egypt, or are working on the banks

L 2

of the river, or are gossiping under the pleasant shade of the palms. The old women are at home minding the babies, or grinding corn, or baking bread. The young girls are busy in the fields picking cotton, or reaping, or sowing the seed for the next harvest. It is at the wayside well that the life of the people may be best seen. A pleasant picture of the groups which gather there has been drawn by Howard Hopley in the *Leisure Hour*.

'We lay hidden one day beneath a screen of intertwisted palm fronds, dreamily lapped in a kind of doze—a slumbrous feeling communicated, I believe by watching the shameful inactivity of a tribe of birds in their twilight cloisters above of boughs swinging gently in the lazy airs of summer's noon,—birds that manifestly toiled not for their living, but took it on trust, flaunting themselves in the most gorgeous plumage imaginable, and neither singing, nor even chatting, for the matter of that. We were lying here, I say, when we espied through our leafy screen the advent of some travellers. A mother and two children—a chubby unclad urchin of two or three, and an elder sister—entered from the outer glare and squatted down in the golden light filtering from above on to the sandy area of the grove. They could not have travelled far, for they came in so gladsome and fresh. The daughter, a fine-grown girl of twelve, ran off to the well and tripped back playfully, with one hand daintily steadying an earthen bowl, dripping over with the grateful drink. Her mother awaited it, her back against a palm, in the attitude of *Judæa Capta* on the Roman coin. How these Nubian faces flash out sometimes an intelligence that no one would give them credit for! This woman, under thirty, perhaps, yet already old and wrinkled, might have been handsome enough once, but the expression of her face was dull and stolid—of the earth earthy. Yet as she sat there straining her little blackamoor to her breast, the soul came up in her face, and she looked positively beautiful. It was like lighting the candle within the lantern. She wore a tunic of camel-hair fabric, Nubian fashion, looped

NUBIAN WOMAN.

up on each shoulder, leaving the arms bare. It had more the cut of the Greek palla, than the skirt of the Egyptian fellah—a kind of extra fold falling from the neck to the waist. The daughter, a pretty little woman, lissom and shapely, you might have taken for a dryad of the wood. Just budding into the woman, she retained all the playfulness of the child, and romped free in the changing leafy lights of this copse, as if her life were all play. There was something so gracious and winsome about her that you could not find heart to cavil. Yet her hair was reeking with castor oil, and I am afraid the gloss on her supple limbs was attributable to that same unguent. She

NUBIAN MUSICIANS.

seemed almost perfect in form; and the hair in question, which fell in a hundred little plaits about her shoulders (shortened in a line across the forehead), framed a face of which the big black eyes, pouted lips, and placid mien, seemed an echo of those sweet faces you see pictured in the old tombs—an echo from a far-back world. Her sole dress, save a necklace or two of beads, was a short petticoat of tiny strips of leather, a kind of fringe decked out coquettishly with a multitude of cowry shells and glass beads, all of which tinkled merrily as she skipped along. You could not, for the life of you, call it an immodest costume, the thing was so natural and innocent. Indeed, in this country, until girls marry, such is their only dress, save a slight veil thrown over the head against the sun.'

Though Nubia did not form part of Egypt proper, yet at the present day it more closely resembles the Egypt of the Pharaohs than does the region of the Lower Nile. Cut off from the rest of the world by the cataract on the north, and by the desert on the east and west, its population has been kept pure from the intermixture of foreign blood, and its manners and customs have remained almost unchanged. Faces are depicted on the monuments which might pass for portraits of those whom we see around us. The contour of the features is precisely the same. This likeness is rendered more obvious by a similarity in the mode of dressing the hair, which is arranged in small corkscrew curls, kept close to the head by saturation with castor-oil. The necklaces, earrings, and bracelets are the same as those worn three or four thousand years ago. In any Nubian hut, wooden pillows or headrests may be found whose form is absolutely undistinguishable from those which may be seen in the British Museum, brought there from Theban tombs.

A ROADSIDE WELL

EGYPTIAN GIRL.   WOODEN PILLOW.

The temples of Nubia are even more numerous than those of Egypt. But being placed there by foreign rulers as trophies of their victories, they have little historical importance, and, except those of Abu-Simbel, present few remarkable features. That of Dandour is of the Roman period, and was founded in the reign of Augustus. It is curious

as an illustration of the way in which classical architects worked upon native models. In some points there is an almost servile imitation of the original, and yet the whole tone and feeling are thoroughly non-Egyptian. It does not need a study of the inscriptions to tell us that, though dedicated to Osiris, Isis, and Horus, the sway of those deities had already passed away.

Though the temple at Dekkeh is but little older than that at Dandour, it has an interesting history. Its *adytum* was built by Ergamun, an Ethiopian monarch, who broke through the barbarous customs of his race and set at defiance the tyranny of the priests. Diodorus tells us that up to this time the priests had always informed the king when the time had arrived for him to die, whereupon, in obedience to their commands, he slew himself. This strange custom seems to have grown out of a feeling, like that which prevailed among our Norse ancestors, that it was disgraceful for a warrior to die from disease or old age, and the *sagas* record several instances of aged chiefs rushing on certain death to escape so dishonourable an end. Sir Gardner Wilkinson points out that a similar custom yet exists amongst certain Ethiopian races which lie farther to the south. Ergamun having received the intimation that the time had come to immolate himself, he not only refused to obey, but collecting

TEMPLE OF DANDOUR.

his troops, marched to the temple, slew the priests, and effected a thorough reform of the whole system. Ergamun clearly distinguished between submission to the priests and reverence for the gods, for he is represented on the walls of the temple as making the accustomed offerings to the deities, and the usual cartouches declare that he was 'protected by Amon,' 'the chosen of Ra,' and 'the beloved of Isis.'

About twenty-five miles above Dekkeh are the remains of a temple belonging to the earliest period, that of Rameses the Great. It is called by the Arabs the Wady Sabooah, the Valley of the Lions, from the avenues of

sphinxes which led up to the propylon in front of the temple. At the
entrance of the avenue stand two colossal statues of Rameses, with sculptures
recording his victories and celebrating his glories. Most of the sphinxes are
buried in the sand which has drifted over them, but their huge heads
protruding
from the plain
have a most
impressive
effect, and fill
with awe the
wandering
Bedouin, who
regard them
as the work
of demons.

Sailing up
the river for
about seventy
miles above
Wady Saboo-
ah, through
ranges of
desert hills,
sloping down
to green
banks, stud-
ded with
palm and mi-
mosa, or
standing cliff-
like over the
stream, we
see before us
a bold mass
of rock upon
which, as we
approach it,
colossal
figures be-

ENTRANCE OF THE TEMPLE OF DEKKEH.

come visible. They are so vast that they look like some freak
of nature rather than the work of puny men. It is Abu-Simbel—
one of the temples of the great Rameses and worthy to rank with
the edifices of Thebes or Gizeh. Elsewhere, the great Egyptian

builders had erected their edifices upon the surface of the earth. Here a mountain had been hollowed into shrines for the gods, and hewed into imperishable monuments of the glory of Pharaoh.

The smaller of the two temples is cut into the rock to the depth of ninety feet. It was dedicated to Athor, the Lady of Aboshek, as she is called. The façade, ninety feet in length, represents Rameses standing among the gods, as though their equal in dignity and power. In the interior, the mild, gentle face of the goddess appears on the walls amongst her kindred deities, whilst

ARABS IN THE WADY SABOOAH.

the hero-king records his conquests of the world as far as it was then
known.

Elsewhere this temple would rivet our attention upon itself: here it is
dwarfed almost into insignificance by its companion. Four granite warders
hewn out of the living rock keep watch at its portals, seated in solemn
majesty, as they have sat for nearly four thousand years. Figures fail to
convey any adequate sense of their magnitude. As given by Murray, their
dimensions are as follows: 'Their total height is about sixty-six feet without
the pedestal; the ear measures three feet five inches; from the inner side of
elbow joint to end of middle finger, fifteen feet. The total height of the
façade of the temple may be between ninety and one hundred feet.' The
lower part of the figures is buried in sand, but they tower so high above

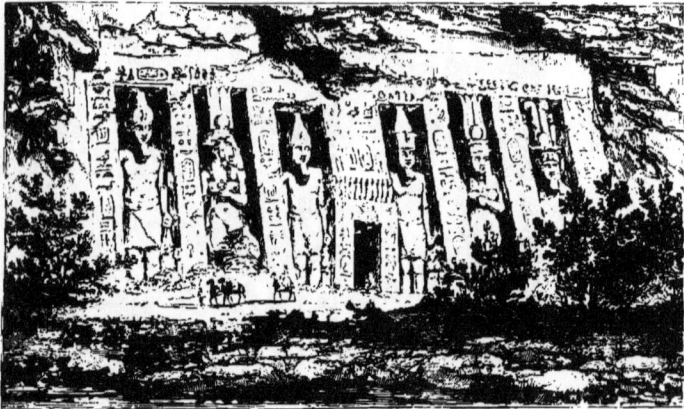

FAÇADE OF SMALLER TEMPLE AT ABU-SIMBEL.

the drifted mass, that it is a task of some labour to climb up into the lap
of one of them.

The beauty of the faces is even more remarkable than their enormous
magnitude. Usually we associate a coarseness and rudeness of finish with
great size in works of art: but every visitor is struck by the delicacy and
expressiveness of the features. One writer speaks of 'the sweet sad smile
of the placid pensive face:' another is fascinated by 'the expression placid
and cheerful—full of moral grace:' a third sees in them 'a dignity and
composure, a tranquil pity, a serene hopefulness more than human:' a fourth
says, 'They are unique in art. The masterpieces of Greece, higher in rank,
have nothing to match with the mystic beauty of these.' There may be

some exaggeration in these words. And yet the solemn expressiveness of these colossi cannot be doubted.

The head of one of the statues is broken off, the other three are tolerably perfect. On the leg of one of them is a curious Greek inscription. Herodotus relates that the troops of King Psammetichus who were stationed at Syene, growing weary and mutinous, deserted, and fled into Ethiopia. They were pursued by order of the king. Two of the soldiers who were sent to bring back the fugitives have here recorded the fact, and given their names— Damearchon and Pelephus —as forming part of the expedition. It is seldom that a historical narrative receives such contemporaneous illustration and confirmation. Still more seldom is it that the bad, though ancient, customof scratching obscure names upon a venerable monument possesses any value whatever.

PART OF FAÇADE OF GREAT TEMPLE AT ABU-SIMBEL.

The mountain behind these gigantic figures is hollowed out to a depth of about two hundred feet. The excavations consist of a grand hall, with eight side chapels opening into it, a second smaller hall, a corridor, and an adytum with altar and figures in relief. The walls are covered with paintings and sculptures, and in the grand hall are eight colossal Osiride columns

twenty feet in height, each standing erect with its back against a square
shaft, thus forming a central aisle. They are all exactly alike, with the
same placid solemn expression as those in the façade. Each is crowned
with the serpent-crested Pshent, and holds in its hands, which are crossed
upon the breast, the crook and flail or scourge, emblems of divine power and
judgment. They are robed from head to foot in the close-fitting tunic or shroud
of death. Round the loins a belt is tied, falling in lappets upon the knee, and
bearing the cartouche of Rameses.

The walls are glowing with colour, like the pages of an illuminated

GREAT TEMPLE AT ABU-SIMBEL.

missal magnified a thousandfold. Their theme is everywhere the same—the
glory of Rameses. We cannot fail, however, to be struck by the contrast
between the tranquil, gentle face of the deified monarch, and the deeds of
savage ferocity which are here ascribed to him. Long lines of captives are
led bound before him on their way to execution. He himself is depicted as
slaying them with a pitiless cruelty. In one sculpture he is grasping by
their hair a group of prisoners, representing the various nations, African and
Asiatic, which he has conquered. With his uplifted sword he is about to
decapitate them. The god Amon hands him a scimitar, in token of his

approval of the deed. We follow the mighty conqueror throughout his campaigns. In one place he is charging in his war-chariot upon a whole phalanx of Scythians. In another, he, single-handed, slays their chief. In a third he is laying waste the territory of the Ethiopians. But everywhere his countenance wears the same expression of tranquillity and repose which nothing can disturb.

The entrance to the temple is so small, that only a feeble ray of light can penetrate, leaving the halls in utter darkness, which is imperfectly dispelled by the aid of candles or torches.[1] But as the opening is towards the

ETHIOPIAN, NEGRO, AND ASIATIC CAPTIVES BEFORE RAMESES.

RAMESES SLAYING A GROUP OF AFRICAN AND ASIATIC CAPTIVES.

east, there are certain seasons of the year at which the light of the rising sun or moon falls full into the vast area. This of course only happens when the point on the horizon at which the luminary rises exactly fronts the entrance, that is to say, twice in the year with the sun, once a month with the moon. Then for a few minutes a beam of light streams through the narrow portal, penetrates the great hall, and finds its way into the very adytum, illuminating

[1] Visitors to Egypt should on no account omit to take with them a plentiful supply of magnesium wire, and an ordinary bull's-eye lantern. The value of the latter for concentrating light on particular points is very great.

as with magical effect the figures there. This innermost shrine was dedicated to the Sun and Moon, whose symbols are over the altar. We may, therefore, conjecture that the internal arrangements of the temple were originally planned so that on the great festivals this impressive spectacle might be witnessed.

At Abu-Simbel our Egyptian tour terminates. We drift slowly down the

MENEPHTAH, THE PROBABLE PHARAOH OF THE EXODUS.

Nile, gliding past the ruins of departed greatness. As we revisit the shattered monuments of the most gigantic system of idolatry which the world has ever seen, the contrast between bygone glory and present degradation is forced upon us. It is impossible to forget that, when Egypt was at the summit of its pride and power, its impending doom was again and again foretold by Hebrew prophets. When Thebes was in her glory, and her subsequent conquerors were only wild hordes of the desert, Joel began the warning:

> ' Egypt shall be a desolation, and Edom shall be a desolate wilderness,
> For the violence against the children of Judah,
> Because they have shed innocent blood in their land.
> But Judah shall dwell for ever, and Jerusalem from generation to generation.' [1]

A hundred years later, Isaiah renewed the burden :

> ' The Egyptians will I give over into the hand of a cruel lord :
> And a fierce king shall rule over them, saith the Lord, the Lord of hosts.
> Surely the princes of Zoan are fools,
> The counsel of the wise counsellors of Pharaoh is become brutish :
> How say ye unto Pharaoh, I am the son of the wise, the son of ancient kings ? ' [2]

The doom was again denounced by Ezekiel, when the destroyer was nearer at hand, yet still before the long and flourishing reign of Amasis :

> ' I am against thee, Pharaoh king of Egypt,
> The great dragon that lieth in the midst of his rivers,
> Which hath said, My river is mine own, and I have made it for myself.
> And all the inhabitants of Egypt shall know that I am the Lord,
> Because they have been a staff of reed to the house of Israel.
> And the sword shall come upon Egypt, and great pain shall be in Ethiopia,
> When the slain shall fall in Egypt, and they shall take away her multitude,
> And her foundations shall be broken down.
> And they shall know that I am the Lord,
> When I have set fire in Egypt, and when all her helpers shall be destroyed.
> Thus saith the Lord God : I will also destroy the idols,
> And I will cause their images to cease out of Noph ;
> And there shall be no more a prince of the land of Egypt :
> And I will put a fear in the land of Egypt, and I will make Pathros desolate,
> And will set fire in Zoan, and will execute judgments in No.
> And I will pour My fury upon Sin, the strength of Egypt :
> And I will cut off the multitude of No.
> And I will set fire in Egypt : Sin shall have great pain,
> And No shall be rent asunder, and Noph shall have distresses daily.
> The young men of Aven and of Pi-beseth shall fall by the sword :
> And these cities shall go into captivity.
> At Tehaphnehes also the day shall be darkened,
> When I shall break there the yokes of Egypt :
> And the pomp of her strength shall cease in her :
> As for her, a cloud shall cover her, and her daughter shall go into captivity.
> Thus will I execute judgments in Egypt : and they shall know that I am the Lord.' [3]

Blended with these denunciations of impending ruin are the promises of a bright and glorious future. As we trace the exact and literal fulfilment of the one, we gain new confidence in the full and final accomplishment of the other. If He ' who delighteth in mercy, and judgment is His strange work,' has not allowed one word of His threatenings to fail, how much more shall His gracious assurances of pardon and restoration be verified ?

---

[1] Joel iii. 19, 20.　　[2] Isaiah xix. 4, 11.　　[3] Ezekiel xxix. 3, 6 : xxx. 4, 8, 13-19.

'In that day there shall be an altar to the Lord in the midst of the land of Egypt,
And a pillar at the border thereof to the Lord.
And it shall be for a sign and for a witness unto the Lord of hosts in the land of Egypt:
For they shall cry unto the Lord because of the oppressors,
And He shall send them a saviour, and a great one, and He shall deliver them.
And the Lord shall be known to Egypt, and the Egyptians shall know the Lord in that day,
And shall do sacrifice and oblation ; yea, they shall vow a vow unto the Lord, and perform it.
And the Lord shall smite Egypt : He shall smite and heal it :
And they shall return even to the Lord,
And He shall be entreated of them, and shall heal them.
In that day shall there be a highway out of Egypt to Assyria.
And the Assyrian shall come into Egypt, and the Egyptian into Assyria,
And the Egyptians shall serve with the Assyrians.
In that day shall Israel be the third with Egypt and with Assyria,
Even a blessing in the midst of the land: whom the Lord of hosts shall bless, saying,
Blessed be Egypt My people,
And Assyria the work of My hands, and Israel Mine inheritance.'[1]

[1] Isaiah xix. 19-25.

RECENT DISCOVERIES IN EGYPT.

CROCODILES ON THE UPPER NILE.

ENTRANCE PASSAGE TO THE EMPTY TOMB OF SETI I.

SECTION IV.

RECENT DISCOVERIES IN EGYPT.

SINCE the first edition of this work was printed, Egyptology has made very great strides. The language is better known, multitudes of papyri, stelae, and inscriptions of various kinds have been translated. We know much more of the social and religious ideas of the marvellous nation who, in the dawn of history, peopled the valley of the Nile. This period has also witnessed some of the most surprising, interesting, and important discoveries of antiquities that have ever been made in Egypt. In the brief limits at our disposal, nothing like a complete sketch of these can be attempted. We can refer at any length to only the most important, viz., the great find at Deir-el-Bahari, and give a hasty glance at a few others.

The most wonderful event in recent Egyptian history is the now world-famous discovery at Deir-el-Bahari in 1881. Prior to the occurrence of the

event, had anyone ventured to assert that the mummy of Thothmes III. would
ever be found, that we should be able to look upon the real face of
Rameses II., the Pharaoh of the Oppression, that, in one great discovery,
we should come upon many of the most famous kings and queens in
Egyptian history, these statements would have been considered entirely out
of the range of probability. Yet all this and more has come to pass.

During the early part of 1881, various reports and rumours were current
relative to a great discovery of antiquities in the neighbourhood of Thebes,
and that the secret, whatever its nature, was the possession of four Arab
brothers named Abd-er-Rasûl, who lived among the rock-cut tombs hard
by the Ramesseum. Professionally these men were guides; actually they
spent most of their time in breaking into tombs and securing mummies,
which, contrary to law, they sold to whomsoever would buy them. Early
in 1881, Maspero caused Ahmed Abd-er-Rasûl to be imprisoned, and for
two months he was shut up at Kench. The monotony of prison life was
varied by occasional bastinado, and by threats of execution if he did not
reveal all he knew. He endured all this, and yet kept right well his secret.
But another brother, named Mohammed, attracted by Maspero's judicious
offer of considerable baksheesh to the man who could and would satisfy his
curiosity, made a clean breast of it, and on July 5th, 1881, led Brugsch Bey,
whom Maspero had sent from Cairo to act for him, to Deir-el-Bahari. How
and when the Arab brethren came upon their find is to this day their own
secret.[1]

After a long climb up the mountain slope, and the scaling of a high
limestone cliff, behind a great rock a shaft about six feet square was found,
which had been sunk some forty feet into the limestone. At the foot of
this a passage ran westwards for twenty-five feet, and then northwards into
the heart of the mountain, terminating in a sepulchral chamber twenty-three
feet by thirteen in extent, and about six feet high.

What followed cannot be better told than in Brugsch Bey's own words.

'Finding Pharaoh,' he told Mr. Wilson, 'was an exciting experience
for me. It is true I was armed to the teeth, and my faithful rifle, full of
shells, hung over my shoulder; but my assistant from Cairo, Ahmed Effendi
Kemal, was the only person with me whom I could trust. Any one of the
natives would have killed me willingly, had we been alone, for every one of
them knew better than I did that I was about to deprive them of a great
source of revenue. But I exposed no sign of fear, and proceeded with the
work. The well cleared out, I descended, and began the exploration of the
underground passage.

'Soon we came upon cases of porcelain funeral offerings, metal and

[1] Most interesting accounts of this event are found in the article called 'Lying in State at Cairo,' by Miss Edwards, in *Harper's Magazine* for July, 1882; and in the articles 'Finding Pharaoh,' by F. L. Wilson, and 'Pharaoh the Oppressor,' by John A. Paine, in the *Century* for May 1887. The Editor received much valuable help from these articles in preparing this section.

alabaster vessels, draperies and trinkets, until, reaching the turn in the passage, a cluster of mummy-cases came into view in such number as to stagger me. Collecting my senses, I made the best examination of them I could by the light of my torch, and at once saw that they contained the mummies of royal personages of both sexes; and yet that was not all.

Plunging on ahead of my guide, I came to the chamber, and there, standing against the walls, or lying on the floor, I found even a greater number of mummy-cases of stupendous size and weight. Their gold coverings, and their polished surfaces so plainly reflected my own excited visage, that it seemed as though I was looking into the faces of my own ancestors. The gilt face on the coffin of the amiable Queen Nefert-ari seemed to smile upon me like an old acquaintance.

'I took in the situation quickly with a gasp, and hurried to the open air, lest I should be overcome, and the glorious prize, still unrevealed, be lost to science. It was almost sunset then. Already the odour which arose from the tomb had cajoled a troupe of slinking jackals to the neighbourhood, and the howl of hyenas was heard not far distant. A long line of vultures sat upon the highest pinnacles of the cliffs near by, ready for their hateful work. The valley was as still as death. Nearly the whole of the night was occupied in hiring men to help remove the precious relics from their hiding-place. There was but little sleep in Luxor that night.

'Early the next morning three hundred Arabs were employed under my

OUTER MUMMY CASE OF QUEEN NEFERT-ARI.

direction—each one a thief. One by one the coffins were hoisted to the surface, were securely sewed up in sail-cloth and matting, and then were carried across the plain of Thebes to the steamers awaiting them at Luxor. Two squads of Arabs accompanied each sarcophagus—one to carry it, and a second to watch the wily carriers. When the Nile overflow, lying midway of the plain, was reached, as many more boatmen entered the service, and bore the burden to the other side. Then a third set took up the ancient freight, and carried it to the steamers. Slow workers are these Egyptians, but after six days of hard labour, under the July sun, the work was finished.

'I shall never forget the scenes I witnessed when, standing at the mouth of the shaft, I watched the strange line of helpers while they carried across the historical plain the bodies of the very kings who had constructed the temples still standing, and of the very priests who had officiated in them —the temple of Hatshepsu nearest; away across from it, Gûrneh; further to the right the Ramesseum, where the great granite monolith lies face to the ground; further south, Medinet Abû, a long way beyond the Deir-el-Medineh; and there the twin Colossi, or the vocal Memnon and his companion; then, beyond all, some more of the plain, the line of the Nile, and the Arabian hills far to the east and above all; and with all, slowly moving down the cliffs and across the plain, or in the boats crossing the sea, were the sullen labourers carrying their antique burdens. As the Red Sea opened and allowed Israel to pass across dry-shod, so opened the silence of the Theban plain, allowed the strange funeral procession to pass,— and then all was hushed again.

'When we made our departure from Luxor, our late helpers squatted in groups upon the Theban side and silently watched us. The news had been sent down the Nile in advance of us. So, when we passed the towns, the people gathered at the quays, and made most frantic demonstrations. The *fantasia* dancers were holding their wildest orgies here and there; a strange wail went up from the men, the women were screaming and tearing their hair, and the children were so frightened I pitied them. A few fanatical dervishes plunged into the river and tried to reach us, but a sight of the rifle drove them back, cursing us as they swam away. At night fires were kindled and guns were fired.

'At last we arrived at Bûlâk, where I soon confirmed my impression that we had indeed recovered the mummies of the majority of the rulers of Egypt during the XVIIIth, XIXth, and XXIst dynasties, including Rameses II., Rameses III., King Pinetem, the high priest Nebseni, and Queen Nefert-ari, all of whom are now at Bûlâk, arranged pretty much as I found them in the long-hidden tomb. And thus our Museum became the third and probably the final resting-place of the mummy of the great Pharaoh of the Oppression.'

On leaving the chamber in the mountain where these mummies had so long reposed—for it was in that very place that Brugsch Bey told Mr. Wilson the story—at the entrance to the shaft the latter photographed the group of which we give here an engraving. It possesses more than passing interest, since it shows the entrance to the shaft; reclining on the right is Professor Maspero, standing in the centre is Brugsch Bey, and the Arab in the foreground is Mohammed Abd-er-Rasûl, holding in his hand the rope by which the mummies of kings and queens and priests who lived from 3,000 to 4,000 years ago, were hauled up from their long-lost tomb.

The following is a list of the mummies of kings and queens removed to Bûlâk, around whom most historic interest centres :—

Mohammed.   Brugsch.   Maspero

MASPERO, BRUGSCH BEY, AND MOHAMMED ABD-ER-RASÛL.

(As photographed by E. L. Wilson at the mouth of the shaft at Deir-el-Bahari.)

King Seke-nen-Râ Ta-âken and Queen Ansera, of the XVIIth Dynasty; Queen Ahmes Nefert-ari, King Amenhetep I., Thothmes II, and Thothmes III., of the XVIIIth Dynasty; Seti I., Rameses II., and Rameses III., of the XIXth Dynasty; Queen Netem-Maut, King Pinetem I., and King Pinetem II. of the XXIst Dynasty.

Some of the sarcophagi of these royal personages are of huge dimensions, the largest being that of Queen Ahmes Nefert-ari. The coffin is ten feet long, made of cartonnage, and in style resembles one of the Osiride pillars of the Temple of Medinet Abû. Its weight and size are so enormous that sixteen men were required to remove it.

Standing near the end of the long dark passage running northward, and not far from the threshold of the vault, lay the sarcophagus of Thothmes III., close to that of his brother Thothmes II. The mummy-case of the latter was in a lamentable condition, and had evidently been broken into and subjected to rough usage. On the lid, however, were recognised the well-known cartouches of this illustrious monarch. On opening the coffin the mummy itself was exposed to view, completely enshrouded with bandages; but a rent near the left breast showed that it had been exposed to the violence of tomb-breakers. Placed inside the coffin, and surrounding the body, were found wreaths of flowers—larkspurs, acacias, and lotuses. The body measured only five feet two inches; so that, making due allowance for shrinking and compression in the process of embalming, still it is manifest that Thothmes III. was not a man of commanding stature, but in shortness of stature as in brilliancy of conquests, finds his counterpart in the person of Napoleon the Great.

Soon after the arrival of these precious relics at Bûlâk, it was thought desirable in the interests of science to ascertain whether the mummy bearing the monogram of Thothmes III. was really the remains of that monarch. It was therefore unrolled. The inscriptions on the bandages established beyond all doubt the fact that it was indeed the most distinguished of the kings of the brilliant XVIIIth dynasty; and once more, after an interval of thirty-six centuries, human eyes gazed on the features of the man who had conquered Syria, and Cyprus, and Ethiopia, and had raised Egypt to the highest pinnacle of her power; so that it was said that in his reign she placed her frontiers where she pleased. The spectacle was of brief duration; the remains proved to be in so fragile a state that there was only time to take a hasty photograph, and then the features crumbled to pieces and vanished like an apparition, and so passed away from human view for ever. Professor Maspero felt such remorse at this result that, for fear of a similar catastrophe, the unrolling of Rameses the Great was delayed until 1886.

Thothmes III. was the man who overran Palestine with his armies two hundred years before the birth of Moses, and has left us a diary of his adventures; for, like Cæsar, he was author as well as soldier. It seems strange that though the body mouldered to dust, the flowers with which it had been wreathed were so wonderfully preserved that even their colour could be distinguished; yet a flower is the very type of ephemeral beauty, that passeth away and is gone almost as soon as born. A wasp which had been attracted by the floral treasures, and had entered the coffin at the moment of closing, was found dried up, but still perfect, having lasted better than the king.

A most interesting account of the mightiest of Egyptian kings is given in Maspero's report of the unrolling of the mummies of Rameses II. and of what had been considered to be the mummy of Queen Nefert-ari, but which turned out to be Rameses III. It is dated June 3rd, 1886, two days only before Maspero resigned his post as Curator of the Museum.

'Bûlâk, June 3. 1886.—The year 1886, the 1st day of June, MM. Gaston Maspero, Director-General of the Excavations and Antiquities of Egypt, Emil Brugsch Bey, keeper, and Urbin Bouriant, assistant keeper, of the Museum of Bûlâk, proceeded, in the hall called "The Hall of Royal Mummies," to unbandage those two mummies which, in the printed catalogue, are numbered 5,229 and 5,233, both being among those discovered in the subterraneous hiding-place at Deir-el-Bahari.

'The mummy (No. 5,233) first taken out from its glass case is that of Rameses II., Sesostris, as testified by the official entries bearing date the 6th and 16th years of the reign of the High Priest Her-hor Se-Amen, and the High Priest Pinetem I., written in black ink upon the lid of the wooden mummy case, and the further entry of the 16th year of the High Priest Pinetem I., written upon the outer winding-sheet of the mummy, over the region of the breast. The presence of this last inscription

THE PROFILE OF RAMESES II.
From a photograph taken at Bûlâk

having been verified by His Highness the Khedive, and by the illustrious personages there assembled, the first wrapping was removed, and there were successively discovered a band of stuff twenty centimètres in width rolled round the body, then a second winding-sheet sewn up and kept in place by narrow bands placed at some distance apart, then two thicknesses of small bandages, and then a piece of fine linen reaching from the head to the feet. A figure representing the Goddess Nut, one mètre in length, is drawn upon this piece of linen, in red and white, as prescribed by the ritual. The profile of the goddess is unmistakably designed after the pure and delicate profile of Seti I., as he is known to us in the bas-relief sculptures of Thebes and

Abydos. Under this amulet there was found another bandage, then a layer of pieces of linen folded in squares and spotted with the bituminous matter used by the embalmers. This last covering removed, Rameses II. appeared. The head is long, and small in proportion to the body. The top of the skull is quite bare. On the temples there are a few sparse hairs, but at the poll the hair is quite thick, forming smooth, straight locks about five centimètres in length. White at the time of death, they have been dyed a light yellow by the spices used in embalmment. The forehead is low and narrow; the brow-ridge prominent; the eyebrows are thick and white; the eyes are

small and close together; the nose is long, thin, hooked like the noses of the Bourbons, and slightly crushed at the tip by the pressure of the bandages; the temples are sunken; the cheekbones very prominent; the ears round, standing far out from the head, and pierced like those of a woman for the wearing of earrings; the jawbone is massive and strong; the chin very prominent; the mouth small but thick-lipped, and full of some kind of black paste. This paste being partly cut away with the scissors, disclosed some much worn and very brittle teeth, which, moreover, are white and well preserved. The moustache and beard are thin. They seem to have been kept shaven during life, but were probably allowed to grow during the king's last illness; or they may have grown after death. The

THE HEAD OF RAMESES II.
(From a photograph taken at Bûlâk.)

hairs are white, like those of the head and eyebrows, but are harsh and bristly, and from two to three millimètres in length. The skin is of earthy brown, splotched with black. Finally, it may be said the face of the mummy gives a fair idea of the face of the living king. The expression is unintellectual, perhaps slightly animal; but even under the somewhat grotesque disguise of mummification, there is plainly to be seen an air of sovereign majesty, of resolve, and of pride. The rest of the body is as well preserved as the head; but in consequence of the reduction of the tissues, its external aspect is less life-like. The neck is no thicker than the vertebral column. The chest is broad; the shoulders are square; the arms are crossed upon the breast; the hands are small and dyed with henna; and the wound in the left side through which the embalmers extracted the viscera, is large and open. The legs and thighs are fleshless; the feet are long, slender, somewhat flat-soled, and dyed, like the hands, with henna. The corpse is that of an old man, but of a vigorous and robust old man. We know, indeed, that Rameses II. reigned for 67 years, and that he must have been nearly 100 years old when he died.

'The unbandaging of the mummy of Rameses II. took less than one quarter of an hour. After a short pause of a few moments, at precisely ten minutes before ten o'clock, the mummy numbered 5,229 was, in its turn, removed from its glass case. It was discovered in the great sarcophagus numbered 5,247, which also contained another mummy in a very dirty and tattered condition. As this sarcophagus bore the name of Nefert-ari, the wife of King Ahmes I. of the XVIIIth Dynasty, it had been taken for granted that No. 5,229 was the mummy of this queen. The other mummy was supposed to be that of some unknown princess who had been laid beside Nefert-ari by the priests employed to conceal the royal mummies in the hiding-place at Deir-el-Bahari. Consigned to the Museum stores, the mummy decayed and gave out so foul an odour that it became necessary to get rid of it. It was accordingly opened, and proved to have been bandaged very carefully; but the body was no sooner exposed to the outer air than it fell literally into a state of putrefaction, dissolving into black matter which gave out an insupportable smell. It was, however, ascertained to be the corpse of a woman of mature age and middle height, belonging to the white races of mankind. There were no traces of writing on the bandages, but a small strip of linen discovered in the sarcophagus No. 5,247 was decorated with a scene of adoration of King Rameses III., in the likeness of two forms of Amen. A short legend, written partly in cursive hieroglyphs and partly in hieratic, states that the piece of linen thus decorated was the gift of the head laundress of the royal household, and it was accordingly supposed that the anonymous mummy was one of the many sisters, wives, or daughters of Rameses III.

'The mummy, No. 5,229, was very neatly wrapped in orange-coloured linen, kept in place by small strips of ordinary linen. There was no outer inscription, but upon the head was a linen band covered with mystical figures.

'M. Maspero here reminded His Highness the Khedive that Nefert-ari is represented upon certain monuments as of a black complexion, while upon other monuments she is seen with a yellow skin, and with the soft hair of an Egyptian woman. Hence there have arisen innumerable discussions among Egyptologists, some affirming that the queen was a negress, while others maintain that the black tint of her face and body was a fiction originating with the priests. The worship of this queen was extremely popular at Thebes, where she was deified under one of the forms of Hathor, the black goddess, the goddess of death and of the shades. The opening of the mummy, No. 5,229, would, therefore, probably settle this historical question for good and all.

'The orange-coloured winding-sheet being removed, there appeared beneath it a white sheet bearing an inscription in four lines :—" The year XIII., the second month of Shomou, the 28th day, the First Prophet of Amen, King of the Gods, Pinetem, son of the First Prophet of Amen, Piankhi, the Scribe of the temple Zoserou-Khonsu, and the scribe of the Necropolis Boutchamou, proceeded to restore the defunct King Ra-user-ma Mer-Amen, and to establish him for Eternity."

'The mummy, which had hitherto been taken for Nefert-ari, was then the mummy of Rameses III.; and the anonymous mummy was without doubt that of Nefert-ari.

GOLD-FACED INNER MUMMY CASE OF QUEEN NEFERT-ARI.

From a photograph taken at Boulak.

'This point being verified, Rameses III. was placed erect and photographed in his bandages. Short as was the delay, it seemed too long for the impatient spectators. The strange revelation, which had substituted one of the great conquerors of Egyptian history for the most venerated queen of the XVIIIth Dynasty, had astonished and excited them to the uttermost. The unbandaging of the mummy then recommenced in the midst of general impatience.

'All had left their places and crowded round the operators. Three thicknesses of bandages were rapidly unwound, then came a casing of sewn canvas covered with a thin coat of cement. This casing being cut with the scissors, more layers of linen appeared. The mummy seemed to diminish and reveal its forms under our fingers. Some of the wrappings were inscribed with legends and groups in black ink, notably the God Amen enthroned, with a line of hieroglyphs below, stating that this bandage was made and offered by a devotee of the period, or, perhaps, by a princess of the blood royal :—" The Lady Songstress of Amen Ra, King of the Gods, Taït-aat-Maut, daughter of the First Prophet of Amen, Piankhi, in order that the God Amen should accord her life, health, and strength."

'Two pectoral ornaments were laid in the folds of the wrappers, one of gilt wood, bearing the usual group of Isis and Nepthys adoring the sun ; the other in pure gold, inscribed with the name of Rameses III. One last wrapper of stiffened canvas, one last winding-sheet of red linen, and then a great disappointment, keenly felt by the operators ; the face of the king was coated with a compact mass of bitumen, which completely hid the features. At 20 minutes past 11 His Highness the Khedive left the hall of mummies.

'The work was resumed in the afternoon of the same day, and on Thursday morning, the 3rd of June, a fresh examination of the bandages revealed inscriptions upon two of them. The first is dated the year IX., the second the year X. of the High Priest Pinetem I. The tarry substance upon the face of the mummy being carefully attacked with the scissors was detached little by little, and the features became visible. They are less well preserved than those of Rameses II., yet they can to a certain extent be identified with those of the portraits of the conqueror. The head and face are closely shaved, and show no trace of hair or beard. The forehead, without being lofty or very broad, is better proportioned and more intellectual than that of Rameses II. The brow-ridge is less prominent, the cheekbones are less high, the nose is less hooked, the chin and jaw are less heavy. The eyes appear to be larger, but it is not possible to be certain of this last point, the eyelids having been removed, and the cavities of the eyeballs having been stuffed with rags. The ears are closer to the head than those of Rameses II., and they are pierced in like manner for the reception of earrings. The mouth is disproportionately wide, and the thin lips reveal a row of white and well-placed teeth. The first molar on the right side appears to have been broken, or to have been worn away earlier than the rest. In short, Rameses III. is like a smaller imitation of Rameses II. The physiognomy is more delicate, and, above all, more intelligent; but the height of the body is less, the shoulders are less wide, and the strength of the man was inferior. What he was himself in his individual person as compared with Rameses II., so was his reign as compared with the reign of Rameses II. His wars were not fought in Syria or Ethiopia, but at the mouths of the Nile and on the frontiers of Egypt. His buildings were of a poor style and of hasty construction. His piety was as pompous as that of Rameses II., but his resources were more meagre. His vanity was, however, as boundless; and such was his supreme desire to copy in all things the example of his illustrious predecessor, that he gave to his sons the names of the sons of Rameses II., and almost in the same order of birth.

'The two mummies, replaced in their glass cases, will henceforth be exhibited with their faces uncovered, like the mummies of King Pinetem and the priest Nebsouni.'

As illustrating yet further the wonderful light this discovery throws upon Egyptian history, we give Maspero's account of the unrolling of the mummies of Sekenen-Rā Ta-āken, a monarch of the XVIIth dynasty, who reigned nearly 1800 years B.C., and of Seti I., the father of Rameses II. Seti holds a very prominent position in Egyptian history. He was a great and successful warrior, and he was the father of Rameses II. Sekenen-Rā is one of the heroes of early Egyptian history. He headed the popular movement against the mysterious Hyksos kings, which, after a struggle extending over 150 years, led to their expulsion from Egypt. He figures as one of the

heroes of an ancient romance written upon a papyrus about the time of the
Exodus, and of which the British Museum possesses a large fragment.
Maspero's report of the unrolling of his body, which took place June 9th,
1886, is very interesting, as illustrative of the details of the battle in which
he lost his life.

'The mummy, numbered 5,227, first removed from its glass case, was
that of the King Sekenen-Rā Ta-āken (XVIIth Theban dynasty), as shown
by the inscription, written in red ink and retouched with the brush, upon
the cover of his mummy case. Two large winding-sheets of coarse texture,
loosely fastened, covered the body from head to foot. Next came pieces of
linen carelessly swathed, and pledgets of rags held in place by narrow
bandages; the whole of these wrappings being greasy to the touch and
impregnated by a fetid odour. The outer coverings removed, there remained
under our hands a kind of spindle of stuff measuring about 1 mètre 82
centimètres in length, and so slender that it seemed impossible there should
be space enough inside it for a human body. The two last thicknesses of
linen being stuck together by spices and adhering closely to the skin, they
had to be cut asunder with a knife, whereupon the entire body was exposed
to view. The head was thrown back, and lying low to the left. A large
wound running across the right temple a little above the frontal ridge was
partly concealed by long and scanty locks of hair. The lips were wide open,
and contracted into a circle, from which the front teeth, gums, and tongue
protruded, the latter being held between the teeth and partly bitten through.
The features, forcibly distorted, wore a very evident expression of acute
suffering. A more minute examination revealed the position of two more
wounds. One, apparently inflicted by a mace or a hatchet, had cloven the
left cheek and broken the lower jaw, the side teeth being laid bare. The
other, hidden by the hair, had laid open the top of the head a little above
the wound over the left brow. A downward hatchet-stroke had here split
off an enormous splinter of skull, leaving a long cleft, through which some
portion of the brain must have escaped. The position and appearance of
the wounds make it possible to realize with considerable certainty all the
circumstances of this last scene of the king's life. Struck first upon the
jaw, Ta-āken fell to the ground. His foes then precipitated themselves upon
him, and, by the infliction of two more wounds, despatched him where he
lay, one being a hatchet-stroke on the top of the head and the other a lance
or dagger wound just above the eye. We already know that Ta-āken fought
against the Shepherds—*i.e.*, the so-called "Hyksos" invaders—who ruled
Egypt for about 500 years, but till now we did not know that he died on
the field. The Egyptians were evidently victorious in the struggle, which
took place over the corpse of their leader, or they would not have succeeded
in rescuing it and in carrying it off the field. Being then and there hastily
embalmed, it was conveyed to Thebes, where it received the rites of sepul-

ture. These facts explain, not only the startling aspect of the mummy, but the irregular fashion of its embalmment. The chest and ribs, unduly compressed by operators working against time, are broken, and present the appearance of a collection of blackened *débris*, interspersed with scattered vertebræ. The pelvis is intact, the bones of the arms and legs are all separate, and decomposition must have already set in before the embalmers began their work. A large white blotch which surrounds the wound on the brow appears to be neither more nor less than a mass of brain substance which has exuded and mortified. Thus hastily embalmed, the mummy was not proof against destructive influences from without. The wrappers are eaten through by worms, and shells of the larvæ of maggots are found in the long hair. Ta-āken was about forty years of age at the time of his death. He was tall, slender, and, to judge by what remains of the muscles of the shoulder and thorax, he must have been a singularly powerful man. His head was small, long, barrel-shaped, and covered with fine black curly hair, worn in long locks. The eye was large and deep-set, the nose straight and broad at the bridge, the cheekbones were prominent, the jaw was massive, the mouth of middle size, somewhat projecting, and furnished with good sound teeth covered with fine enamel. The ears are gone, and there are scarcely any signs of beard or moustache. Ta-āken had been shaved on the very morning of the battle. Take him altogether, he must have been singularly like the Barabras (Nubians) of the present day, and have belonged to a race less mingled with foreign elements than that of the Rameses family.

THE HEAD OF SETI I.
(From a Photograph taken at Bulak.)

'The mummy-case No. 5,232 contained the mummy of Seti I., second king of the XIXth dynasty, and father of Rameses II., as testified by the official entries of the year VI. and XVI. of Hrihor, and the year X. of Pinotmou I., inscribed upon the lid. The arrangement of the various winding-sheets and bandages was the same as upon the mummy of Rameses II. At about midway of the total thickness of the wrappings there occurred two lines of hieratic inscription in black ink, stating that "in the year IX., the second month of Pert (the season of seed-time), the sixteenth day, was the day of re-clothing the King Men-māt-Rā (Seti I.), to whom be life, health, and strength." Another inscription, written on one of the smaller bandages, adds that the linen used for the king's wrappings was supplied by the First Prophet of Amen Menkhopirri in his VIth year ; so giving the date of the latest restoration of the king's funerary trappings. The body presents much the same appearance as that of Rameses II. It is long, fleshless, of a yellow-black colour, and has the arms crossed upon the breast. The head was covered with a mask of fine linen, blackened with bitumen, which it was necessary to remove with the scissors. M. Alexandre Barsanti, upon whom that delicate operation devolved, removed this shapeless mass, and brought to view the most beautiful mummy-head ever seen within the walls of the Museum. The sculptors of Thebes and Abydos did not flatter the Pharaoh when they gave him that delicate, sweet, and smiling profile which is the admiration of travellers. After a lapse of thirty-two centuries, the mummy retains the same expression which characterised the features of the living man. Most striking of all, when compared with the mummy of Rameses II., is the astonishing resemblance between the father and son. The nose, mouth, chin—in short, all the features—are the same; but in the father they are more refined, more intelligent, more spiritual than when reproduced in the son. Seti I. is, as it were, the idealised type of Rameses II. He must have died at an advanced age. The head is shaven, the eyebrows are white, the condition of the body points to considerably more than three-score years of life, thus confirming the opinion of the learned, who have attributed a long reign to this king. The body is healthy and vigorous, not withstanding the knotty state of the fingers, which bear evident traces of gout. The mouth is filled with some kind of paste, but the two teeth which are visible are white and well preserved.'

In addition to engravings of Seti and Rameses we give one of Pinetem II., whose mummy was also found at Deir-el-Bahari. It is interesting from the fact that this king belonged to the XXIst dynasty, which flourished some three hundred years after the XIXth and that the features show the Nubian type.

THE HEAD OF PINETEM II.
From a photograph taken at Būlāk.

As the original tombs of many of these great kings have long been known, and also known to be empty, the reason has been sought why the mummies of these great rulers, belonging to several widely-separated epochs—Sekenen-Rā being as far distant from Pinetem II. as William the Conqueror from William III.—were all brought together into the secret place at Deir-el-Bahari, and when they were put there. Inscriptions upon the mummies show that from time to time properly appointed officials visited the royal mummies, and reported upon their condition. The kings and queens found, down to, and including Rameses III., seem to have been originally buried in their own royal tombs. The tomb in which they were found appears to have been the family vault of the Her-Hor dynasty. Towards the close of the XXth dynasty Egypt fell into a state of considerable social disorder and insecurity. One of the many forms in which crime flourished was the robbing of tombs. From time to time the mummies of the ancient kings were placed in tombs less easy of access than their own, and thus more secure against the assaults of robbers, and at last—when, no one can say—found a permanent refuge in the tomb which, contrary to ancient Egyptian custom, the Her-Hor family made the sepulchre, not only of the monarch who hewed it out, but also of his descendants.

In 1882 a few scholars interested in the study of Egyptian antiquities formed a society, based upon the model of that which has done so much for Palestine, and called it the Egypt Exploration Fund. The object for which subscriptions are sought is the excavation of promising sites in Egypt, and the publication of the results of the work done. The society has kept itself well before the public since its foundation, and some of its discoveries have formed the theme of considerable discussion. It has been subjected to the criticism of being somewhat hasty in jumping to conclusions, and that its memoirs not unfrequently contain statements, identifications and translations that sometimes do not very successfully stand the test of severe examination. But any society doing such good work as the excavation of Egyptian sites deserves support. To get the excavation done is most important, even if the first impressions about the treasures discovered have to be modified later on.

ENTRANCE TO THE TOMB OF SETI I. IN THE VALLEY OF THE TOMBS OF THE KINGS AT THEBES.

The chief results of the work done by the officers of the Fund at Tel-el-Maskhutah and Tanis have already been referred to upon pages 25 and 26 of this volume. During 1885 and 1886 Mr. Flinders Petrie has discovered and explored the sites of Naukratis, and at Tel Defenneh, about sixteen miles from Tanis, of Pharaoh's House in Tahpanhes. The Fund have issued a Memoir on the former, which is a most interesting discovery. The latter will come home more closely to all students of the Bible, inasmuch as it reveals to us the site of an unusual and important conjunction of events in the history of Egypt, Palestine, and Babylonia. Granting that Mr. Petrie is correct in identifying ruins of a massive quadrangular building

N

at Tel Defenneh, the 'Pelusiac Daphnæ' of the Greek writers, with the palace of Pharaoh at Tahpanhes, we have recovered the place whither the daughters of Zedekiah fled, whither Jeremiah himself came, whither also came Nebuchadnezzar, by whom, in all probability, the place was destroyed. This discovery throws considerable light upon the historical events described in Jeremiah xxxvii.-xlvii.

M. Naville has also investigated the ruins and cemeteries at Tel-el-Yahudeyeh, twenty-two miles north-east of Cairo, and inclines to the belief that it was the site of the city of Onia, founded by the Jewish High Priest Onias, about 163 B.C.

The combined results of excavations carried on in Egypt, the more accurate translation of documents and monuments, and the careful investigation of the history and literature of Egypt, are now enabling us to form much clearer and much more accurate ideas about the people themselves, their wonderful story, their complex religious system, their social customs, and the part they have played in the development of mankind. The more fully we can get to understand the history and beliefs of the Egyptians, the more clearly shall we be able to discern their influence upon the still more marvellous history of that people, among whom in the fulness of time came He 'who His own self bore

HEAD OF QUEEN NEFERT-ARI, WIFE OF RAMESES II.
(From a sculpture at Abu Simbel.)

our sins in His body on the tree,' and who died that He might 'gather together in one the children of God that were scattered abroad.'

THE SUEZ CANAL.

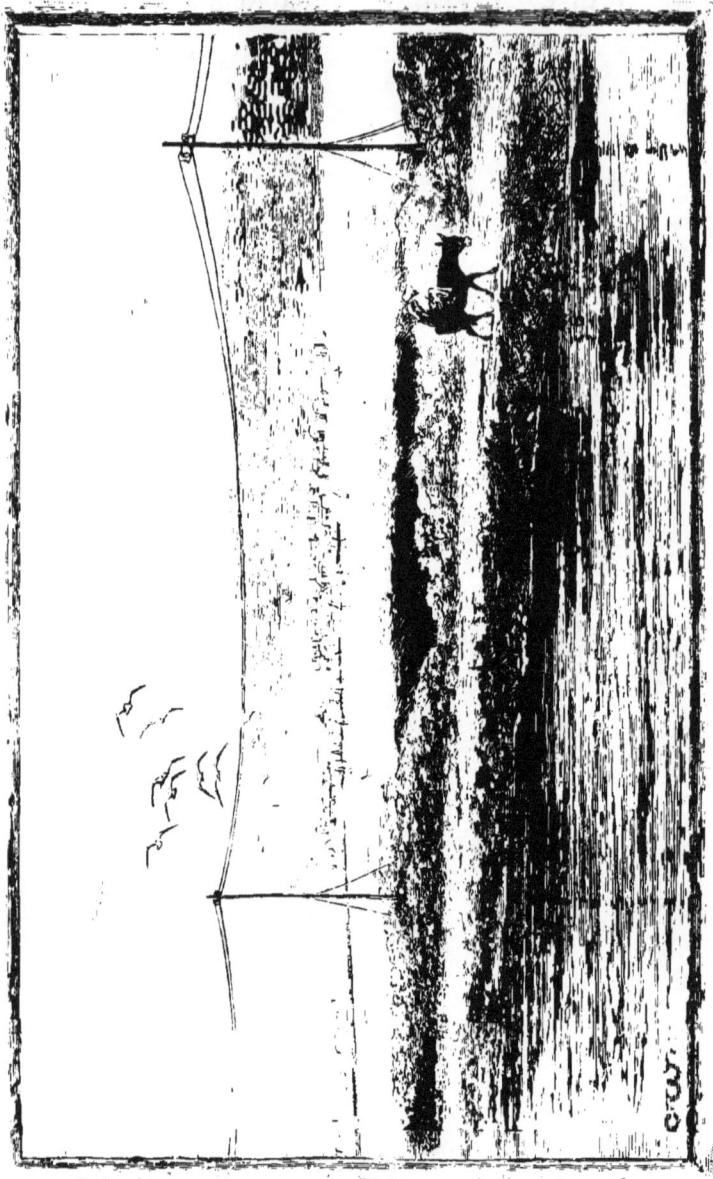

VIEW OF SUEZ FROM THE CANAL.

M. LESSEPS.

SECTION V.

THE SUEZ CANAL.

THE separation of the African Continent from that of Asia, and the formation of a direct waterway between the Atlantic and the Indian Oceans by cutting the Isthmus of Suez, has been often and justly spoken of as one of the most daring achievements of the present century. With less justice is it adduced to prove our immense superiority over ancient engineers in works of great public utility. The canalisation of the isthmus is no modern project. It had been commenced whilst the Israelites were yet in Egypt, and probably formed part of their labours at the period of the Exodus. It was carried forward almost to completion by Pharaoh Necho, who defeated King Josiah in the great battle of Megiddo.[1] And a hundred years later it was finished by the Persian conquerors of Egypt.

It would, however, be an error to suppose that M. Lesseps and his associates simply inherited the ideas of the Pharaohs. The Suez Canal was designed solely to facilitate communication between the Eastern and the Western Continents. For this purpose all that was needed was the construction of a channel wide and deep enough for ocean-going steamers,

[1] 2 Chronicles xxxv. 20-24.

through the narrow neck of land which divides the Mediterranean from the Red Sea, thus avoiding the long *détour* by the Cape of Good Hope. But the ancient Egyptians were not a maritime people. To navigate the Nile was enough for them. A mere ship canal was worthless to a nation which had no foreign commerce, and it might indeed be used for the invasion of their territory by a seafaring enemy. Their canal had to serve, therefore, other purposes than those contemplated by M. Lesseps.

We have already seen that the north-eastern frontier of ancient Egypt was the one most exposed to assault. Once in their history, hordes of nomads poured across the isthmus and established themselves as rulers of the land. By the same route came Idumæan and Canaanitish merchants to exchange their commodities for those of the Nile Valley. The monuments afford innumerable illustrations of this, and the histories of Joseph and his brethren show the nature and extent of the traffic thus carried on. It was therefore important that a line of fortified posts should be constructed to guard this frontier against invasion, and at the same time to protect the caravans from the attacks of marauding Bedouin. But food and water were needful for the labourers employed in the work of construction, for the garrisons who held these outposts, and for the traders who met there to transact their business. These supplies could not be found in the desert. A canal, therefore, was excavated at least as early as the time of Rameses the Great, to convey the waters of the Nile to these points. The sand of the desert, which looks so hopelessly barren, only needs water to make it ‘rejoice and blossom as the rose.’ But sea water, of course, will not serve the purpose. It would only increase, if that were possible, the sterility which already existed. It must be fresh water. This being conducted by canals from the Nile, and running through the eastern wilderness, added a new province to Egypt, and turned the arid waste into a fertile garden. The great Bahr Yûsef, as it is now called, which runs the whole length of Egypt from Cairo to Farshût, offered a barrier to the inroads of Bedouin horsemen, or, if they made their way across it, they were in danger of being cut to pieces before they could effect a retreat. What had proved so serviceable as a defensive work along the Libyan frontier would be even more important on the north-east, from which more serious danger was apprehended. The canalisation of the isthmus by the ancient Egyptians was mainly designed to attain these three ends —to reclaim and fertilise a portion of the desert, to facilitate the construction and maintenance of fortresses on the exposed frontier, and to form a foss as a protection against Bedouin forays. The opening up of a waterway for sea-going vessels was a subordinate purpose, which only took effect at a comparatively recent period in the history. These facts being borne in mind, we shall be able the more easily to understand what follows.

We read that the Israelites ‘built for Pharaoh treasure cities, Pithom and Raamses.’ These were two of the fortresses to which reference has just been made. The former of them is mentioned by Herodotus. The probable ruins of the latter were discovered in 1883 with the statue and cartouche of the great monarch who founded it. The site is covered deeply with desert sand ; but traces of an ancient canal are distinctly visible, which we may fairly conjecture to have been excavated by the labour of the Hebrew slaves who built Raamses and Pithom for the king. Greek and Roman writers ascribe the construction of this canal to Rameses the Great, known to them as Sesostris. This, it will be observed, affords an incidental corroboration to the statement of Scripture ; for the city and the canal were doubtless the work of the same monarch who gave his name to the outpost upon which the Hebrews were at work at the time of the Exodus. Though

LINE OF ANCIENT CANAL IN THE DESERT.

the term 'treasure city' conveys a false impression to our minds, it is not therefore inaccurate. It was not a place in which the royal treasure was deposited, but a fortified khan, where merchants could store their goods and transact their business in safety.

The canal thus commenced, prior to the Exodus, was still further extended by Pharaoh Necho, in the fifth or sixth century before the Christian era. He is the only Egyptian monarch whose name appears in connection with maritime enterprise. In his zeal for the promotion of navigation, he projected the formation of a ship canal connecting the Nile with the Red Sea. Herodotus tells us that one hundred and fourteen miles of this great work had been completed when he was warned by the oracle to desist. This admeasurement is evidently an excessive one. It probably includes the whole distance from sea to sea, without making allowance for the branch of the Nile north of Bubastis, where the canal commenced, or the Bitter Lakes, which lay in its course. The statement of Pliny is probably nearer the truth. He gives it as fifty-seven Roman, equal to sixty-two English, miles. The oracle called upon the king to suspend his operations, on the ground that he was 'working for the barbarians.' This reason has been rejected as absurd by recent historians. But it really was a piece of shrewd advice. The canal, if completed as proposed, would have afforded facilities for the invasion of Egypt by the war-galleys of the Persians, with which the Egyptians could not cope.

About a hundred years later, when the Persian conquerors had succeeded for a time to the throne of the Pharaohs, Darius, the son of Hystaspes, resumed the work commenced so long before. He cleared out the canal, which had begun to silt up, and carried it forward to where Suez now stands. When the Persian and Egyptian empires had succumbed to the military prowess of the Macedonian conqueror, and the power of the Greek dynasty had been consolidated in Egypt, Ptolemy Philadelphus (B.C. 250) widened and deepened the waterway, reconstructed the portion at the southern end, and completed the undertaking upon so grand a scale that vessels of war could enter the Nile from the Mediterranean, and sail into the Gulf of Suez without difficulty. Under the Romans, as might be expected from the character of the people, the repairs and extensions necessary from time to time were carried out, so as to maintain this important line of communication unbroken. In the anarchy and confusion which followed upon the downfall of the Roman empire, all the public works were allowed to fall into dilapidation. The canals were choked up, and remained unnavigable till the Arab conquest of Egypt. Under the vigorous administration of Amrou they were reopened. Corn and other provisions were conveyed along them for the use of Mecca, Medina, and other Arabian towns. This continued, with some interruptions, for about three hundred and fifty years. Since that time they have been altogether neglected, though their course can yet be traced through the desert, and they have been to some extent utilised for the construction of the ship canal.

From this brief summary it will be seen that the canalisation of the isthmus is no new project. It was commenced more than three thousand years ago, and two thousand years have elapsed since it was completed from sea to sea. During the French occupation of Egypt, at the commencement of the present century, the project of reopening this ancient channel of communication suggested itself to the mind of Napoleon. Surveys were made, and plans prepared by his orders. But the ambitious schemes of the emperor having been baffled by the battle of the Nile, nothing further was done, and the proposal remained in abeyance.

The various engineers who had turned their attention to the subject prior to M. Lesseps proposed to adopt, with some modifications, the plan followed by the ancient Egyptians, and construct a fresh-water canal by tapping the Nile somewhere in the Delta. Many high authorities are of opinion that he erred by deciding upon a different course.

Mr. Barham Zincke thus sums up the argument in favour of the scheme which was rejected : ' The ancient Egyptians would have decided in favour of fresh water, because they could then have constructed it at half the cost ; and would, furthermore, by so doing, have had a supply of water in the desert, sufficient for reclaiming a vast extent of land, which would have more than repaid the whole cost of construction. Instead of cutting a canal

ZAGAZIG, ON THE FRESH-WATER CANAL.

deep in the desert at an enormous cost, they would, as it were, have laid a canal on the desert. This they would have done by excavating only to the depth requisite for finding material for its levées and for the flow of the water which was to be brought to it from some selected point in the river. It is evident that this kind of canal might have been made wider and deeper than the present one at far less cost. The river water would then have filled the ship canal, just as it now does the sweet-water canal parallel to it. The sweet-water canal now reaches Suez. A sweet-water ship canal might have done the same. As far as navigation is concerned, the only difference would have been that locks would have been required at the two extremities, such as Darius and Ptolemy had at Arsinöe. These locks would have been at Suez, and the southern side of Lake Menzaleh.

But the diminution in the cost of construction, say £8,000,000, instead of £16,000,000, would not have been the chief gain : that would have been found in the fact that the canal would have been a new Nile in a new desert. It would have contained an inexhaustible storage of water to fertilise, and to cover with life and wealth, a new Egypt."

The fresh-water canal, the construction of which was an essential pre-liminary to commencing the main work, leaves the Nile near Cairo, and pursues a north-easterly course till it reaches the site of Pithom, where, as we have seen, the Hebrews were labouring at the period of the Exodus. It thence runs due east to Ismailia, the central station on the ship canal, and is continued southward to Suez. Pumping-engines at Ismailia force the water along iron pipes northward to Port Saïd, a distance of about fifty miles. Reservoirs are constructed at all the principal stations along this part of the canal for the supply of the inhabitants, and open drinking-troughs are placed at distances of about three miles from each other along the line, which are kept constantly full, by means of an ordinary ball and cock, like those in use in our English cisterns.

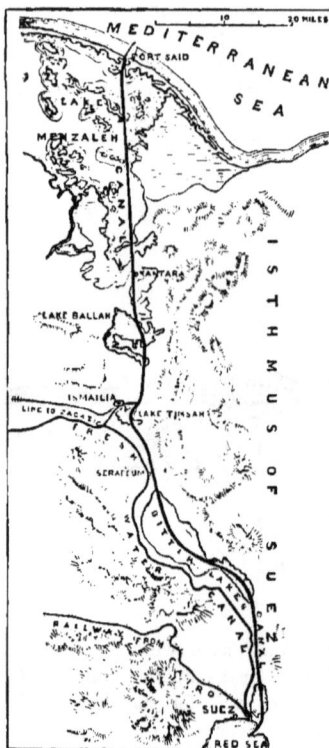

The ship canal is as nearly as possible one hundred miles in length, running due north and south from Port Saïd to Suez. It was not found necessary, however, to excavate the channel for the whole distance. A glance at the map will show that it runs through four great lakes : Menzaleh, Ballah, Timsah, and the Bitter Lakes. The first two of

MAP OF THE CANAL.

these, with only a few short cuttings, extend for 41 miles, the second for 5, the third for 25, making together about 60 miles, and leaving 40 miles of earth-work to be excavated. Lake Menzaleh was so near the Mediterranean as to be always under water. The others were deep depressions in the soil, marking the spots where lakes of sea water were left when geological changes raised this part

¹ *Egypt of the Pharaohs and the Khedive*, p. 420.

of the isthmus above the level of the Gulf of Suez. It was only necessary, therefore, to admit water into them, to bank the channel, and to make it of the required depth by dredging.

At Suez, the works of the canal consist chiefly of an entrance channel into the Red Sea, increasing gradually from 72 feet in width at the bottom, to 980 feet of a basin or dock, and a considerable quantity of reclaimed land. But at Port Saïd the works are on a much more important scale. The water was so shallow that within a mile and a half of the shore there was not sufficient depth to float the vessels which would pass through the

PORT SAÏD.

canal. Hence it has been necessary to construct two walls or breakwaters; one, of the enormous length of 2730 yards, and a shorter one 2070 yards long. These breakwaters are not built in the solid fashion of those at Plymouth and Cherbourg, but are composed of blocks of concrete which have been manufactured at Port Saïd out of lime brought from Europe and sand obtained on the spot. These blocks—which weigh about twenty tons apiece, and 25,000 of which have been required—have been tumbled down roughly one upon another and allowed to settle by their own weight. Between these two rude walls a passage of depth sufficient for large ships has been dredged, but the alluvium brought down through the adjacent mouths of the

Nile, which formerly was deposited without hindrance over the whole of the surrounding coast, is now stopped by the most westerly of the breakwaters, and has not only formed large accumulations of solid shore on its outside, but has forced its way through the interstices of the blocks into the passage intended for ships.

The accumulation of mud at the mouth, and of drifting sand along the course of the canal, involves the necessity of constant dredging. The

CARAVAN STARTING FROM SUEZ.

expense which has thus to be incurred, together with the enormous amount of capital sunk in the construction of this great work—about seventeen millions sterling—have hitherto prevented its being a great financial success. But the continuous increase in the number and tonnage of the vessels which pass along it, make it probable that ultimately it will be as remunerative to the shareholders as beneficial to the world at large.

There is little to interest the traveller in a voyage through the canal. From the deck of one of the large ocean steamers, an extensive view is

gained over the expanse of desert on either hand. But passing through it
as I did, in one of the Viceroy's steam launches, nothing is seen but a long
monotonous line of sand-banks, which slope upwards from the water's edge
and obstruct the view. Where the canal passes through the Bitter Lakes
and Lake Timsah, the eye can range over the lagoons, but they offer
nothing to attract attention except flocks of birds—pelicans, flamingoes,
herons, cranes, and ducks apparently in infinite numbers. After a sojourn in
Egypt, even these have become so familiar as no longer to excite interest.
It was at first thought that sharks and fishes from the Red Sea and the
Indian Ocean would pass along the canal into the Mediterranean. They

KANTARAH, NEAR THE JUNCTION OF THE CANAL AND LAKE MENZALEH.

are, however, kept back by an unforeseen cause. The evaporation in the
broad open lagoons is so great that the water in them becomes nearly as
salt as that in the Dead Sea. Fish which are only accustomed to water
whose density and saltness is that of the ocean, find this an insuperable
barrier to their farther progress, and the shores were at first lined with their
dead bodies. It is said that a few varieties are becoming familiarised to
their new *habitat*, and are thriving in it. But none of the larger and more
important species have, as yet, made their way through the intensely salt
waters of the Bitter Lakes.

Ismailia, the central station on the canal, is admirably adapted for a
sanatorium, and was designed for this by the engineers of the company. It

combines the pure, dry, exhilarating air of the desert with splendid sea-bathing, and irrigation from the fresh-water canal produces the most luxuriant vegetation in the gardens and pleasure-grounds around it. The town was laid out upon a pretentious scale. Here are boulevards, open squares, promenades, the *Grande Rue de l'Empereur*, the *Boulevard de l'Impératrice*, and all the high-sounding titles of a French city. M. Lesseps has a charming residence, and the Viceroy a palace, in the suburbs. But the scheme is a failure. The houses are empty and falling into ruins. The hotel is without guests. Visitors do not arrive, and vessels sail past without stopping. But its advantages as a health resort are so great that it may even yet realise the hopes of its founders.

The only point of historical interest on the canal is Kantarah. Lying just at the southern end of Lake Menzaleh, it marks the route by which travellers have always passed to and fro between Egypt and Palestine. Millions of warriors have trodden these sands age after age, from the time when Rameses crossed the isthmus for the invasion of Assyria and Scythia, to that of Omar, when the Moslem conquerors, emerging from their Arabian deserts, wrested their richest province from the enfeebled hands of the Byzantine Emperors, or of Napoleon, whose troops, parched with thirst, broke their ranks to pursue the mirage of the desert. 'The father of the faithful' and his descendants came hither on their way to Egypt, when the famine was 'sore' in the land of Canaan. The 'Midianites merchantmen,' coming 'from Gilead with their camels bearing spicery and balm and myrrh, going to carry it down to Egypt,'[1] bore past this spot their young Hebrew prisoner to sell him into slavery. But no army, however laden with the spoils of victorious war ; no caravan, however enriched with the accumulation of successful commerce, can so fire our imagination or fix our thoughts as the two poor fugitives, who, weary and footsore, fled across this dreary waste, escaping with 'the young Child' from the wrath of Herod the king.[2] The glory of God, the salvation of man, the sole hope of a ruined world, had been committed to their charge. He who was carried in His mother's arms or walked with infant feet over this oft-trodden track, had stooped to mortal weakness that we might rise to a glory which shall never pass away.

---

[1] Genesis xxxvii. 25.   [2] Matthew ii. 13-21.

EGYPT TO SINAI.

Plain of Er Kháil, Sinai, showing the Convent.

CROSSING THE DESERT.

SECTION VI.

EGYPT TO SINAI.

THE traveller in Egypt or Palestine finds himself everywhere surrounded by the traces of a long and diversified series of events of the utmost interest and importance. Commencing with the very dawn of history, they continued to run their course, not merely for centuries, but for millenniums, and have been recorded on imperishable monuments, or in yet more imperishable writings. The ever varying aspects of nature in those countries serve to illustrate and explain the great drama of their history. We can see how the course of human affairs was modified or determined by the conditions of physical geography. The sea, the rivers, the mountains, the desert, all had their influence upon the development of the Hebrew and the Egyptian people, and were employed for the accomplishment of His purposes, by Him who 'hath made of one blood all nations of men for to dwell on all the face of the earth, and hath determined the times before appointed, and the bounds of their habitation.'[1]

Lying between these two countries—between them, not only geographically but historically—is a district which is in striking contrast to both. The Sinaitic peninsula was the route by which the Israelites passed from Egypt

---

[1] Acts xvii. 26.

O

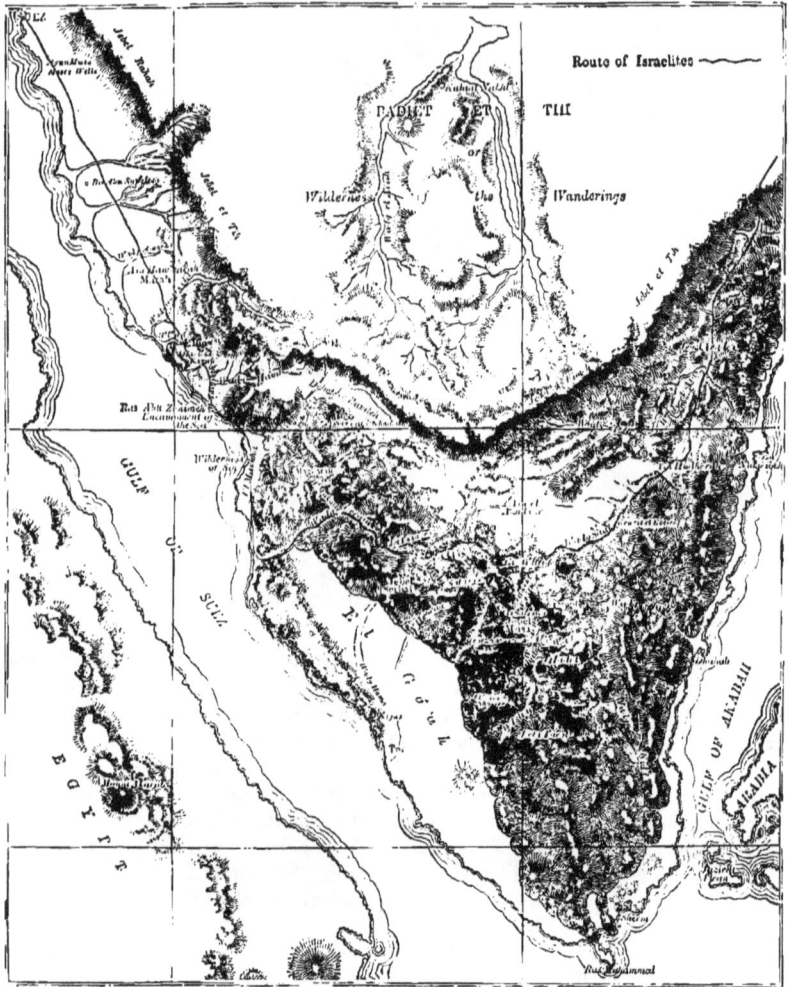

THE SINAITIC PENINSULA.

into Palestine, and it formed the birthplace and cradle of the nation. They
entered it a horde of fugitive slaves. They left it fused and welded into an
organic whole, which continues down to our own day. And it is this

solitary fact which gives to it its sole claim on our attention. A solemn and impressive monotony is the characteristic of the region. History records but a single event. Nature offers but a single aspect unchanged from age to age. At certain seasons of the year 'a thin and transparent veil of greyish green ' is drawn over portions of the soil. Here and there a clump of palms, tamarisks, and acacias may be found. A few wells of bitter, brackish water attract the wandering Bedouin with their flocks and herds. We shall, hereafter, see reasons for believing that at the period of the Exodus the population of the peninsula was more numerous, and its soil somewhat more fertile, than now. But with these exceptions it is 'a waste howling wilderness' of bare rocks, intersected by *wadies* of sterile sand, gravel, and marl, without history and without change.

In attempting to trace the route of the children of Israel from Egypt to Sinai, we are beset by difficulties which almost preclude the possibility of a definite or satisfactory conclusion.

We have already seen that the boundary line between Egypt and the desert is uncertain and fluctuating, dependent not on fixed and natural, but on varying and artificial, conditions. It is determined by the energy with which irrigation is carried out. The conflict between the fertilising river and the encroaching sand—between Osiris and Typhon, as the old mythology symbolised it,—is conducted with ever varying alternations of victory and defeat. Under the Pharaohs and the Ptolemies, canals had pushed the frontier of Egypt forward into districts which are now utterly desolate and barren. Recent discoveries enable us to fix, with tolerable certainty, the site of Raamses, which formed the starting-point of the Exodus. But at the present day Raamses lies outside the limits of cultivation, and is buried beneath the sands of the desert. Where was Succoth--*the shepherds' booths*—which formed the first halting-place ? And where was ' Etham, which is in the edge of the wilderness ?'[1] In the changed condition of the country we can discover no premisses to warrant a positive conclusion as to these important sites. The question is still further complicated by geological changes in the isthmus. The Red Sea formerly extended much farther to the north than at present. An upheaval of the soil has cut off the district now known as the Bitter Lakes from the head of the Gulf of Suez. And there is some evidence to prove that this upheaval has taken place at a period subsequent to the Exodus. It is then possible, perhaps even probable, that Pi-hahiroth, Migdol, and Baal-zephon must be sought for, not where the present coast line of the Red Sea would indicate, but many miles to the north of where the town of Suez now stands. After a careful balancing of the arguments adduced by Egyptologists and Biblical expositors, I come to the conclusion that this is the case. Without presuming to dogmatise upon so difficult and complicated a problem, the theory which

[1] Exodus xii. 37 ; xiii. 20. Numbers xxxiii. 5 7.

places the line of transit through the sea somewhere near Shaloof, a station on the canal, about fifteen miles north of Suez, seems to me to have the greatest weight of evidence in its favour.[1] We thus adopt the cogent arguments of Brugsch and others as to the line of route, and escape the difficulty of supposing, with them, that the passage was through the Serbonian Bog, or the Bitter Lakes, instead of through the sea, as the narrative evidently requires.

A yet further difficulty in the way of tracing the course pursued by the fugitives arises from the character of the only historical document we possess on the subject. The Mosaic narrative is one of remarkable precision and accuracy. It is in fact an itinerary giving the journeys day by day, and the halting-places night by night.[2] But, as Dean Stanley has remarked, it was written by and for those who were so well acquainted with the localities that they required no explanatory details. The names being familiar and the places known, no further indication was thought needful. This, whilst it affords a strong incidental corroboration of the authenticity of the narrative, deprives us of those helps to identify the stations on the route which might otherwise have been afforded. The names having disappeared, or being only handed down by doubtful and obscure traditions, we are left to work out a conjectural line of march from insufficient data.

But whatever perplexities we may feel in the endeavour to trace the precise course followed by the Israelites, the general outlines of the scenery remain unchanged, and we can realise with the utmost vividness and certainty the general aspect of the country through which they passed. The Sinaitic peninsula is divided into two main portions. The northern, known as the Badiet et Tih, or *Desert of the Wandering*, is a vast triangular plateau of limestone, which runs down to a point in the centre of the peninsula. It has no marked features and no historical associations. Notwithstanding its name, we have no evidence that the Israelites actually crossed it, though in the course of their forty years' wanderings they may have done so. On their journey southward from Egypt to Sinai, they kept along its western edge between the Jebel et Tih and the Gulf of Suez, and on their northward journey from Sinai to Canaan they skirted its south-eastern corner. Separated from this northern plateau by a belt of sand, the

---

[1] Professor Hull, the head of the geological expedition sent out to this region by the Palestine Exploration Fund in 1883, confirms this view. He says (*Mount Seir*, page 37): 'The waters of the Red and, I may add, the Mediterranean Sea, extended over the lands of Egypt and along the shore of the Gulf of Suez to a height of over two hundred feet above the present level of these waters, at a time when the existing species of shells were already living. The process of elevation of this sea-bed over so large a tract was probably exceedingly gradual, and at the date of the Exodus the elevation may not have taken place up to the present extent. A strip of Red Sea water—not very deep—may at this time have stretched from the Gulf of Suez as far north as the Great Bitter Lake, forming to the host of Israel an effective barrier to their progress into the desert. The passage may have taken place to the north of the present head of the Gulf of Suez.'

See also the chapter, 'The Geography of the Exodus,' in Sir William Dawson's *Egypt and Syria*, By-Paths of Bible Knowledge, No. VI.

[2] Numbers xxxiii. 5-37.

Debet er Ramleh, and stretching
away in the south, is a chaos of
mountain peaks — sandstone and
granite—some of which rise to a
height of nearly 9000 feet. In win-
ter the higher summits are capped
with snow. With this exception, they
are for the most part absolutely
bare. The splintered savage tors,
denuded of soil, have been compared
to a sea running mountains high
and suddenly petrified into solid
immovable masses. Tempests of
frightful violence often rage among

MOUNT SERBAL.

them. Lightning leaps from crag to crag. Peals of thunder seem to shake
the earth. Torrents of rain descend, and, forming cascades, sweep all before
them with destructive fury. The *wâdies* or valleys which intersect these
mountain ranges are covered with marl or gravel, generally strewn with
granite boulders. Clumps of broom, acacia, willow, tamarisk and wild
palm, with here and there a cypress, are found springing from the arid
soil. Sage and other aromatic shrubs afford a meagre pasture for the
camels, flocks, and herds of the Bedouin. Wells or pools of brackish water
are not infrequent. And there are a few oases where the date-palm grows

WELLS OF MOSES.

luxuriantly along the banks of some running stream which wells forth from
a cleft in the rocks, but is soon absorbed by the thirsty earth. This sparse
and meagre vegetation, however, is not sufficient to dissipate the general
aspect of barrenness and desolation which the wilderness presents.

Following in the track of the Israelites, we leave Suez, and in about
three hours reach the Ayûn Mûsa, or Wells of Moses. These wells are
of all shapes and sizes. Some are merely shallow pools, others are deep
shafts lined with masonry. In most of them the water is bitter and acrid ;
in a few only is it drinkable. Aquatic plants cover the surface of the
ponds, and the surrounding soil is laid out in gardens which are irrigated

by sakiehs like those used in Egypt. If we adopt the theory that the passage of the Israelites through the Red Sea was at a point to the north of the present head of the Gulf, Ayûn Mûsa may with some probability be identified as Marah, 'where they could not drink of the waters, for they were bitter.'[1]

The route southward from Ayûn Mûsa leads along the shore over gravelly plains many miles broad, which slope upward from the sea to the mountains of the Tîh. After heavy rains the stiff tenacious marl is pitted with numerous pools of water, and is sprinkled with the aromatic shrubs

WÂDY GHARANDEL.

which constitute the flora of the desert. But the scorching sun soon dries up the pools, and the short-lived plants wither into dust. Several wells of bitter water are passed, each of which has been fixed upon as Marah, according to the view taken of the place of passage. About fifty miles south of Ayûn Mûsa the Wâdy Gharandel is reached.[2] The entrance into the

---

[1] Exodus xv. 23.

[2] It was in a valley running down from the Tîh, not far from Ayûn Mûsa, that Professor Palmer and Lieutenant Gill were murdered by the Arabs in 1882. Many are of opinion that the deed was due to orders issued by Arabi Pasha.

valley, or wády, is not much over eighty feet wide, and on either side grey-
looking cliffs of gritstone rise with ragged faces to a considerable height.
But that which adds so great a charm to the scene is an actual stream of
water, rippling along, silvery and bright, garnished on each bank with
luxuriant plants that thrive and flourish in the wet sand. Forget-me-nots
peep out from amidst the sedgy grass reeds and mint that tower above the
water; while some kind of brook plant, like a tangled mat, spreads itself

RUINS AT SERABET EL KHADIM.

over the sandy edges of the rivulet, and sends its long arms, tufted with
rootlets at every joint, out into the running water. Here the vegetation
takes quite a different character. The spiny acacia, the *sumt* of the Arabs,
probably the tree of the ' burning bush ' and the shittim wood of the tabernacle,
grows plentifully; but, spiny though it be, it has to bear its burden of
climbing plants, being generally quite hidden beneath their twisting, rope-like
branches. Conspicuous amongst the larger plants is the *retem* or wild broom,
handsome alike in growth and foliage. It is probably the shrub beneath
which Elijah slept in his wanderings.[1]

          [1] 1 Kings xix. 4.

Date-palms of strangely stunted stature are scattered along the sandy banks; one might readily mistake them for giant yuccas at a hasty glance, so much do they resemble those plants in their mode of growth. These may truly be called '*wild palms:*' dwarfed, and unaltered by man's hand. Was this the memorable place where 'there were twelve wells of water and threescore and ten palm trees'—the veritable Elim of the Exodus? Many travellers believe this wâdy to be the place.'

Striking eastward up the wâdy we soon reach the traces of mines worked by the ancient Egyptians. Hieroglyphic tablets are found in considerable numbers, one of which contains the name of Cheops, the builder of the Great Pyramid, and some are said to be even earlier. At Serabet el

SINAITIC INSCRIPTIONS.

Khadim, which seems to have been the capital of the mining district, are some remarkable ruins, consisting of a temple, the remains of houses, and perhaps a necropolis. Fragments of columns, blocks of stone, pieces of rude sculpture, and mounds of broken pottery lie scattered about in perplexing confusion. The upright blocks or stelas are amongst the most curious parts of the present ruin. They are from eight to ten feet in height, rounded at the top, and fairly well faced. The rock from which they are hewn is a compact sandstone, and they do not appear to be distributed with any regard to uniformity of distances or position. Thickly covering both sides are hieroglyphic inscriptions. This is but one of the many traces of ancient settlements to be found in this part of the peninsula, which seem clearly to

' Exodus xv. 27.

prove that it must have been more thickly populated, and therefore more fertile, in former ages than at present. It is important to bear this fact in mind, as it confutes one of the main arguments brought by infidels against the truth of the Mosaic narrative. Where, it has been asked, could pasture have been found for the 'flocks, and herds, and very much cattle' brought up by the Israelites out of Egypt, and which served for sacrifices

SINAITIC INSCRIPTIONS.

in the wilderness?[1] Whence came the Amalekites and other nations who fought against Israel, and threatened to destroy them?[2] These sceptical questions, like others of a similar class, are based upon an entire misapprehension of the facts. We only need more accurate knowledge to discover a triumphant answer. That the general aspect of the desert must always have been what we now see is indeed certain. But no less certain is it that the oases which still exist were once far more numerous, fertile, and densely populated than now.

In the same district is the Wâdy Mokatteb, or the Written Valley, so called from the number of rude inscriptions and sculptures with which the rocks are covered. They are not peculiar to this valley, but are found in many other parts of the Sinaitic range. They always occur in the lines of route along which caravans of traders or bands of pilgrims are likely to have passed, and are inscribed in the soft sandstone rock which forms the fringe of the harder granite in the centre of the peninsula. The sculptures are grotesque representations of birds, camels, asses, horses, ibexes, and other animals. The inscriptions are sometimes in Greek, Latin, or Hebrew, but more commonly in a character unlike that of any known language. Up to a recent date, the several opinions held regarding the origin of these writings resolve themselves into two: the one that they were the work of the Israelites during

[1] Exodus xii. 38; xxiv. 5.   [2] Exodus xvii. 8-15.

their sojourn in the desert; the other that they were the pastime of Christian shepherds who were permanent residents, or possibly of Christian pilgrims in search of Mount Sinai. This *quæstio vexata* was settled by the discoveries of the late Professor Palmer, who showed that the character is simply 'another phase of that Semitic alphabet whose forms appear alike in the Hebrew, Arabic, and Greek,' or, as it may be explained in other words, constitutes an intermediate link betwixt the Cufic and ordinary Hebrew. Professor Beer refers to a stone in Wâdy Mokatteb on which there was a *bilingual* inscription; Mr. Palmer also discovered it, and states that there can be no doubt that the Greek and Sinaitic writing of which the inscription consists was executed by the same hand. Nor is this a solitary instance. These writings, hitherto supposed to be of so great an age, are only detached sentences, in an Aramæan dialect, 'a great many of them being proper names, with here and there introductory formulæ such as Oriental peoples have been from time immemorial accustomed to prefix to their compositions.' They were probably the work of pilgrims and traders during the earlier part of the Christian era, or for two or three centuries before it. The Christian signs employed denote that many of the inscribers were Christians; but there is evidence to prove that a large proportion of them were Jews or Pagans. 'The writing must have extended into the monkish times, possibly until the spread of El-Islám brought the ancestors of the present inhabitants, Bedouin hordes, from El-Hajaz and other parts of Arabia Proper, to the mountains of Sinai, and dispersed or absorbed that Saracen population of whom the monks stood in such mortal dread.'

Leaving the Wâdy Mokatteb by a boulder-strewn valley, we enter the Wâdy Feiran, the most beautiful and fertile of all the wâdies in the peninsula—perhaps the only one to which these epithets can properly be applied. Some years ago it was devastated by a frightful inundation caused by storms of unusual violence in the mountains, which turned the wâdy into a torrent ten feet in depth. Thirty Bedouin were drowned, hundreds of sheep and goats perished, and upwards of a thousand palm trees were uprooted and washed away. Many years must pass before the traces of this destructive deluge have disappeared.

At the entrance of the wâdy are the remains of some of those ancient buildings to which reference has already been made. Stone circles, and kist-vaens, curiously like those of our own early Celtic period, have been discovered. In some of the latter, opened by Mr. Lord, the bodies were found with the knees bent upon the chest, as was the case in all the tombs of this class examined by him throughout the peninsula. The significance of this fact will be understood by the students of pre-historic antiquities. In and around many of the graves flint implements have been found in considerable numbers, but none were seen in the Wâdy Feiran. About seven miles beyond these ruins the wâdy expands, while the rocks are lower, with wider watercourses intersecting their escarpments. Scrubby little date-palms begin to appear on the patches of alluvium, as if placed there to mark the frontier between sterility and verdure. Farther on, acacias and tamarisks, with palms of more stately mien, can be descried, resembling in the distance a coppice on a sandy plain. Several species of birds flit from bush to bush, some of them warbling as sweetly as an English song thrush; the drowsy hum of insects falls pleasantly on the ear, while the eye experiences a delicious relief in resting upon the deep green foliage of the leafy trees.

A Bedouin settlement is now reached, occupied throughout the year by a number of slaves employed in cultivating the soil, and gathering and preparing the fruit of the date palms. Many of them are negroes, others are of a lighter complexion, with thinner lips and less prominent cheek-bones. Their Bedouin masters visit the spot at intervals to feast upon the products of this delightful oasis, which consist not only of dates, but grain, cucumbers, gourds, pomegranates, and lotuses, as well as large quantities of sugar-cane and tobacco.

FLINT IMPLEMENTS FROM THE SINAITIC PENINSULA.

A narrow rocky gorge having been passed, we enter a sandy plain sparsely covered with stunted tamarisk bushes. On the slopes of the hills are seen ruins of ancient dwellings, proving the existence of numerous inhabitants at some former period. Here a magnificent view is gained of the grandest of all the mountains of the peninsula, Jebel Serbal. Seen from this spot, it presents to the eye of the observer a confused mass of peaks of varying heights, but in reality these are reducible to five well-marked ones, the others being more or less simply accessories. The mountain is composed of granite, and the peaks shoot up precipitously from the basement like so many columns.

Turning a sharp angle of rock which juts out far enough into the wâdy to hide the upper palm-grove, a wonderful scene of enchantment suddenly bursts upon the view. On each side, and to all appearance completely shutting in this part of Wâdy Feiran from the world beyond it, immense

Mount Serrat.

cliffs of bare granite rock seem to tower up into the very clouds. Beneath the shadows of these frowning precipices a vast plantation of date palms flourishes in the richest luxuriance. Through the centre of the grove a rivulet of sparkling water trickles along, anon eddying mysteriously beneath the gnarled roots of a patriarchal pine, as though coyly hiding, but soon dancing out again to the music of its own murmuring ripple. The 'laughing water' rushes past the tangled clusters of wild mint, coquetting with the blue forget-me-nots, kissing the green fronds of the dangling sedge grass, then·tumbling at last in a miniature cascade over a low ledge of rock, is sucked up and consumed by the thirsty sand of the desert. Along the banks of sand and alluvium through which the water has cut a wide channel, grow waving groups of tamarisk trees, while in the patches of cultivated

THE WÂDY FEIRAN.

ground the rich crimson blossoms of the pomegranate eclipse all beside in splendour of colour.

Feiran is clearly a modernised form of the ancient Paran—the surrounding wilderness being so-called from this, the most important settlement in it—but as the name is applied in the Bible to the whole district stretching in a north-easterly direction to the borders of Canaan, it is difficult to fix upon any special site. The magnificent mass of Serbal which arises above the wâdy has been by some writers identified with Sinai—the Mountain of the Law—but upon insufficient grounds. This question will be discussed hereafter in connection with Râs Sufsâfeh and Jebel Mûsa. With more probability the site of Rephidim has been sought in this valley. Here the Amalekites would be likely to make a stand for the defence of the most fertile spot in their territory. The fact that Serbal was a sacred mountain in very early times, and a place of pilgrimage and Pagan worship, gives point to the

statement that Moses, with Aaron and Hur, 'went up to the top of the
hill,' to pray, whilst the battle was raging in the valley, and explains the
language of Jethro: 'Now know I that Jehovah is greater than all gods.'
On the very spot where these idol deities were worshipped, the servants of
the Lord call upon Him for help, and He proves His power by giving
them the victory. [1] The only objection to this identification arises from the
want of water. [2] The difficulty, however, is not insuperable. We may
suppose, either that the host had only reached the lower part of the valley,
which is barren and waterless, whilst the Amalekites barred the progress
upward, or that, in a season of drought, the usual abundant supply had
failed, as often happens in the present day.

THE CONVENT, SINAI.

'And they departed from Rephidim, and pitched in the wilderness of
Sinai, . . . and there Israel encamped
before the mount.' [3] If Feiran is
rightly identified as Rephidim, the route
of the Israelites would be by the
Wâdy esh Sheikh. This is a broad and noble valley shut in by mighty hills,
and in many parts shadowed by groves of tamarisk trees. Its southern
extremity opens into the Wâdy ed Deir, which runs to the south-west, and
forms a right angle with the great plain Er Râhah. This is probably the
wilderness of Sinai spoken of in the quotation just given from the Book of
Exodus. The wâdy turns sharply to the right, and is contracted to a narrow
gorge between the mountains. About half-way up this gorge is the monastery
of St. Catherine, as it is commonly called, though really it is dedicated to

[1] Exodus xvii. 8-15; xviii. 11.   [2] Exodus xvii. 1-6.
[3] Numbers xxxiii. 15. Exodus xix. 1, 2.

the Transfiguration. Its ordinary name is due to the traditional tomb of the saint which it contains.

The convent was founded by Justinian (A.D. 527), and was originally higher up the side of the mountain, perhaps even on the summit. It now lies at the base of Jebel Músa, in a narrow part of the valley surrounded by gardens, which are cultivated by the monks and their Arab servants. Until recently it resembled a beleaguered fortress rather than a convent. The only admission to it was gained by means of an aperture high up in the wall. Visitors were hoisted up by means of a crane, the windlass being worked by the monks inside. The most dignified personages had thus to submit to be treated like bales of goods. Recently the Bedouin, having become friendly with the monks, and the number of visitors having increased, a gateway has been opened, though the strong iron-clamped door is still jealously guarded.[1]

As the sale of manna forms an important item in the income of the monastery, this seems the proper place to inquire whether what now passes under that name is really the same with the manna of the Israelites. That it is the same, and that the miracle consisted in an enormous increase of the quantity produced, has been maintained by many high authorities, against whom the charge of rationalism cannot be urged.[2] The sweet honey-like taste, the whitish colour, the similarity of the name,

SUPERIOR OF THE CONVENT.

and the fact that it must be collected before sunrise, after which time it hardens, or altogether disappears, have been adduced in proof of this conclusion. But the preponderance of opinion is on the other side, and in favour of the view that the manna was not merely increased, but absolutely produced by miracle.

The various legendary marvels which the monks here, as everywhere

---

[1] It was in this monastery that Tischendorf discovered in 1844 some fragments of an ancient Greek MS. of the Bible. In 1859, travelling under the patronage of the Emperor of Russia, he was presented with the priceless treasure of the Codex Sinaiticus, the oldest extant MS. of the New Testament.

[2] For a very elaborate and able discussion of the whole subject, see Ritter's *Geography of Palestine and the Sinaitic Peninsula* (vol. ii. pp. 271-292).

throughout the East, have accumulated around their convent, need not detain us long. A glance will suffice for the tomb of St. Catherine and the shrine of the Burning Bush—the bush still growing out of the soil! All our interest is concentrated upon the one great event of the desert, the manifes-

tation of the Deity to Moses and the camp of Israel. The traditional peak is Jebel Mûsa, which rises to the height of 2600 feet above the convent, 7375 above the level of the sea. There are two roads to the summit. One, constructed some years ago by Abbas Pasha, winds round the

ENTRANCE TO THE CONVENT, SINAI.

mountains and is available for camels. The old road is much rougher and steeper, but is far more interesting. Ascending by the former, a gradual slope leads upward for some distance from the convent for about two hours. Here a curious basin hollowed out of the rock is shown as the foot-print of Mohammed's

JEBEL MÛSA.

camel! From this point the track becomes narrower and steeper, in one place passing through a narrow gap between granite rocks only a few feet wide. A flight of rude stone steps now conducts to the actual summit, where a Christian church and a Mohammedan mosque stand side by side. The view is grand and impressive, ranging over a vast chaos of bare desolate

INTERIOR OF THE CONVENT, SINAI.

peaks; but it is difficult to convince oneself that this can be the scene of the giving of the law. No plain is visible in which the tribes could have encamped in the 'wilderness before the mount.' The Wâdy Sebâiyeh has been pointed out as answering to the requirements of the narrative, but it is too narrow and restricted in area, too rough and boulder-strewn, to have answered the purpose.

Descending by the steeper and older road, we pass, not far from the summit, a magnificent cypress tree towering up amongst the rocks. This is alleged to mark the spot where the Lord appeared to Elijah in fire and storm and earthquake, and spoke to him in 'a still small voice.'[1]   Close by it is a chapel dedicated to the prophet, and said to be built over the cave to which he had retired.   Leaving the plateau on which the chapel stands, we make our way through a narrow path in the rocks, over a flight of rugged broken steps, the road twisting through clefts and chasms and under crags in a bewildering manner, till we come suddenly upon a remarkable archway constructed of blocks of granite.   Here, and at another similar archway a little lower down, the monks used to stand to shrive and absolve the pilgrims on their ascent, before they were permitted to tread the holy ground.   Various legendary shrines and a spring of deliciously clear cold water, encircled by a luxuriant growth of maiden-hair ferns, are passed in the steep descent, and at length the convent is safely reached.

A Monk of the Convent, Sinai.

Rejecting the claims of Serbal and of Jebel Mûsa to be regarded as the Mountain of the Law, the question recurs—can any peak be pointed out which does fully and completely satisfy the requirements of the narrative? There can, I think, be no doubt as to the answer. We have but to re-ascend the mountain as far as the chapel of Elijah, and then, instead of climbing to the peak of Jebel Mûsa, bear away to the north-west over some broken ground and through a series of ravines to reach the summit of Râs Suf-sâfeh.   Here the great plain of Er-Râhah stretches away immediately below us, affording ample space for the hosts of Israel to encamp, whilst the mountain is exposed to view from summit to base.   The narrative, if read from this point, becomes perfectly clear.   Each detail in the text finds its corresponding feature in the land-scape.   Every traveller admits, that if this be not the Mountain of the Law, no other spot can be found more suitable in every respect.   I again avail myself of the admirable summary given by Mr. Lord, whose experience as an accomplished naturalist, geologist, and traveller gives his opinion great weight.

[1] 1 Kings xix.

Rás SgeSáeil and Plain of Eg-Ráĥail.

'Having described the two mountains Jebel Serbal and Jebel Mûsa, it appears to me that neither the one nor the other harmonises with the account of the law-giving as we read it in Exodus. First of all, an immense plain must have spread out before the mount—"and there Israel camped before the mount." Now, taking into consideration the number of people there were with their flocks and herds, a very wide extent of open space was necessarily required for the encampment; but nowhere round Serbal is such a space to be found. Wâdy Alêyat is only a gorge completely filled with immense boulders, and it would be practically impossible for any large concourse of people to encamp in it, in front of Mount Serbal. Magnificent in all its barren immensity as Serbal unquestionably is, still its very height tells against its identity with Scripture narrative. The loudest sounds produced on the summit of the mountain would be but feebly heard, if they could be distinguished at all, by any persons at the base. And from Wâdy Alêyat, or indeed from any of the wâdies round about Serbal, only a very small part of the mountain can be seen.

'As regards Jebel Mûsa, the same objections may be advanced. There is no plain anywhere round it which can be seen from the mount, or upon the expanse of which an immense host of people could "pitch" before the mountain. Wâdy Sebâiyeh is the only wâdy traceable from the top of the

ARCHWAY ON MOUNT SINAI.

mountain which could in any way be regarded as the spot of the encampment; and this falls so short of one's anticipations as to immediately suggest that it cannot be the scene described in Scripture. This impression is even more strongly confirmed when walking through the wâdy, for it then appears utterly impossible to obtain there the required space for a huge encampment.

'As neither Jebel Serbal nor Jebel Mûsa in any way accord with the Mosaic description of the "Mountain of Deliverance," my readers may very naturally ask, Is there not some other mountain in the Sinaitic group that better answers to the description given in the Bible? My reply is, Yes;

and let me explain that I am simply stating the impression made upon my own mind, after a careful inspection of all the mountains constituting the upper group.

'There is a granite hill, not of any great altitude as compared with either Jebel Mûsa or Jebel Serbal, but still rising 2000 feet above the plain of Er-Râhah, from which, if we steadily survey the scene which opens out right in front, we are at once struck with its resemblance to the place we have so often read of and pictured to our imagination. In the one direction, Wâdy-es-Sheikh stretches away to the right as far as the eye can scan the distance, like an immense level valley shut in by walls of mighty granite rocks ; while almost in front Er-Râhah, more like a broad plain than a wâdy, opens out into an expanse of yellow sandy ground, free from rock or boulder, that comes right up to the very foot of the mountain, and trends away into lateral wâdies and gorges also as far as the range of vision can follow it. At a glance from the top of Râs Sufsâfeh you see space enough and to spare, level and sandy, for the hosts of Israel twice told to "pitch" on. Moreover, this space is in front of the mount ; and I am quite sure that any person could be heard in the plain below if shouting loudly from the top of Râs Sufsâfeh. Indeed, during the stillness of the evening, when I have been wandering over the sandy plain of Er-Râhah, the calls of the Arab boys and girls, collecting their goats and sheep from amongst the dry watercourses and gorges of Râs Sufsâfeh, have come pleasantly to my ear. This mountain I am speaking of was immediately in rear of our tents, and forms, as it were, the point of a ledge of loftier hills that in jagged outlines and cloven sides become gradually mixed up with and lost in the yet mightier mountains behind them. It would not be very difficult for the united energies of a goodly host to set "bounds" which should keep the multitude from pressing too closely upon or "touching the mount." And so vast an extent of open unbroken plain, the like of which I did not see on any other part of the peninsula, would have afforded ample space for the people at any time "to remove and stand afar off."

'Another point connected with Sufsâfeh as giving probability to its rank and title to be considered the "Mount Sinai," is that persons coming down through the narrow clefts of the mountain to reach the plain would most assuredly hear the sounds of shouting and singing before they could catch sight of the people from whom the sounds came. "And Moses turned, and went down from the mount, and the two tables of the testimony were in his hand."[1] "And when Joshua heard the noise of the people, as they shouted, he said unto Moses, There is a noise of war in the camp."[2] Again, in the 18th verse, Moses replies and says, "The noise of them that sing do I hear," and then we read that as he suddenly came nigh unto the camp, he saw the golden calf, and the dancing, and then, and not until then, the tables are

[1] Exodus xxxii. 15.   [2] Exodus xxxii. 17.

flung upon the ground, and dashed into fragments "beneath the mount." This hearing voices before the plain could be reached or seen is precisely what would happen at this very day, supposing two or three persons were making their way down from the summit of Mount Sufsâfeh to reach either one of the lateral gullies which lead out into the plain, and at the same time supposing a great tumult to be raging upon Er-Râhah. Now this would be impossible in coming down from Jebel Mûsa, firstly because there exists no plain near its base, and secondly, because the only open ground near the foot of the mount is visible at nearly every point of the descent; and this objection has equal force when applied to Serbal.

' Then we are told in Ex. xxxii. 20 : " And he took the calf which they had made, and burnt it in the fire, and ground it to powder, and strawed it upon the water, and made the children of Israel drink of it." I have already said that there was no stream flowing near Jebel Mûsa ; hence it does not harmonise with the above account. At Jebel Serbal there certainly was a tiny rivulet, but almost inaccessible, except by hard climbing; and being so shut in by masses of granite rock it would prove a matter of impossibility for any number of persons to reach it at a time or drink from it, granting they did get to its brink. But at Sufsâfeh there was a good-sized stream percolating down through the gorge of Lejah, which actually lost itself in the sands of Er-Râhah, and might well have stood for the brook upon the surface of whose waters the fragments of the golden calf were sprinkled.'

EGYPT, SINAI, CANAAN ! The typical and spiritual significance of the histories which these names embody, have been perceived by the Church in every age. Volumes have been written to illustrate and enforce the lessons taught us by the House of Bondage, the Miraculous Deliverance, the Wilderness of Wandering, the Mountain of the Law, and the Promised Land. May we lay to heart one of these lessons inculcated by inspired teaching :

' Ye are not come unto the mount that might be touched, and that burned with fire, nor unto blackness, and darkness, and tempest, and the sound of a trumpet, and the voice of words ; which voice they that heard intreated that the word should not be spoken to them any more : . . . . . but ye are come unto Mount Sion, and unto the city of the living God, the heavenly Jerusalem, and to an innumerable company of angels, to the general assembly and church of the firstborn, which are written in heaven, and to God the Judge of all, and to the spirits of just men made perfect, and to Jesus the mediator of the new covenant, and to the blood of sprinkling, that speaketh better things than that of Abel. See that ye refuse not Him that speaketh. For if they escaped not who refused Him that spake on earth, much more shall not we escape, if we turn away from Him that speaketh from heaven.' '

[1] Hebrews xii. 18-25.

SCOTCH FISHER-FOLK.

SCOTTISH PICTURES. *DRAWN WITH PEN AND PENCIL.*
By SAMUEL G. GREEN, D.D.
Illustrated by Eminent Artists. Imperial 8vo., handsomely bound, gilt edges, 8s.; morocco elegant, 25s.

HAMMERFEST HARBOUR.

NORWEGIAN PICTURES. *DRAWN WITH PEN AND PENCIL.*
With a Glance at Sweden and the Gotha Canal.
By RICHARD LOVETT, M.A.
New Edition, revised and partly re-written. Imperial 8vo., 8s., cloth boards, gilt edges.

RUNNING THE LACHINE RAPIDS.

CANADIAN PICTURES. *DRAWN WITH PEN AND PENCIL.*

By the MARQUIS OF LORNE, K.T.

With numerous Illustrations from Objects and Photographs in the possession of, and Sketches by, the **MARQUIS OF LORNE, SIDNEY HALL,** etc.

ENGRAVED BY EDWARD WHYMPER.

Imperial 8vo., elegantly bound in cloth, gilt edges, 8s. ; morocco, elegant, 25s.

A NATIVE ENCAMPMENT IN QUEENSLAND.

AUSTRALIAN PICTURES. *DRAWN WITH PEN AND PENCIL.*

By HOWARD WILLOUGHBY, of "The Melbourne Argus."

WITH A LARGE MAP AND 107 ILLUSTRATIONS FROM PHOTOGRAPHS AND SKETCHES, ENGRAVED BY E. WHYMPER AND OTHERS.

Imperial 8vo., 8s. cloth boards, gilt edges ; or 25s. in morocco. elegant.

3

SEA PICTURES.

Drawn with Pen and Pencil. By James Macaulay, M.A., M.D., Editor of the "Leisure Hour."

Imperial 8vo., handsomely bound, gilt edges, 8s.; morocco elegant, 25s.

CLOVELLY.

ENGLISH PICTURES.

DRAWN WITH PEN AND PENCIL.

By the Rev. S. MANNING, LL.D.,
and
Rev. S. G. GREEN, D.D.

With Coloured Frontispiece and Numerous Wood Engravings.

RUSSIAN SLEDGING AND COURSING.

RUSSIAN PICTURES. *Drawn with Pen and Pencil.*

By THOMAS MICHELL, C.B., Author of "Murray's Handbook to Russia," etc.

With three Maps, and upwards of one hundred Engravings.

Imperial 8vo. 8s. cloth boards, gilt edges ; morocco, 25s.

ST. OUEN, ROUEN.

LUTHER'S HOUSE, FRANKFURT.

FRENCH PICTURES.

DRAWN WITH PEN AND PENCIL.

By the Rev. Samuel G. Green, D.D. With upwards
of 150 Fine Engravings.

Imperial 8vo., elegantly bound in cloth, gilt edges, 8s. ; morocco, 25s.

PICTURES FROM THE GERMAN FATHERLAND.

Drawn with Pen and Pencil. By the Rev. Samuel G.
Green, D.D. Profusely Illustrated with superior
Engravings.

Bound in handsome cloth boards, full gilt, 8s. ; morocco, 25s.

RUINS OF A SYNAGOGUE AT SHILOH.

THOSE HOLY FIELDS.

Palestine Illustrated by Pen and Pencil. By the Rev. Samuel Manning, LL.D.
With Numerous Fine Engravings.

Imperial 8vo., elegantly bound in cloth, gilt edges, 8s.; morocco, 25s.

COLUMNS OF TEMPLE AT LUXOR.

THE LAND OF THE PHARAOHS.

Including a Sketch of Sinai. By the Rev. Samuel Manning, LL.D. New Edition, revised, and partly
re-written by Rev. R. Lovett, M.A. With Numerous Fine Engravings.

Imperial 8vo., elegantly bound in cloth, gilt edges, 8s.; morocco, 25s.

Indian Pictures.

DRAWN WITH PEN AND PENCIL.

By the Rev. WILLIAM URWICK, M.A.

PROFUSELY ILLUSTRATED BY ENGLISH AND
FOREIGN ARTISTS.

*Imperial 8vo., handsomely bound, gilt edges, 8s. ;
morocco, elegant, 25s.*

SACRED TANK AND TEMPLE, MADURA

NIAGARA BRIDGE.

AMERICAN PICTURES.

DRAWN WITH PEN AND PENCIL.

By the Rev. SAMUEL MANNING, LL.D.

Profusely Illustrated in the best style of Wood Engraving
by eminent English and Foreign Artists.

*Imperial 8vo., elegantly bound in cloth, gilt edges, 8s. ;
morocco, 25s.*

www.ingramcontent.com/pod-product-compliance
Lightning Source LLC
Chambersburg PA
CBHW030734280326
41926CB00086B/1412